HOW TO LOVE AND

Dr Paul Hauck received his Ph.D. from the University of Utah in 1953, and now practises as a clinical psychologist in Rock Island, Illinois, USA. He lectures widely on various aspects of psychology and his writing includes over thirty articles for professional journals. Born in 1924, he is married with three children.

How to Love and be Loved is a welcome addition to his other helpful books published by Sheldon Press: *Calm Down*, *Jealousy*, *Depression*, *How to Do What You Want to Do*, *How to Stand Up for Yourself*, *Making Marriage Work*, *How to Bring Up Your Child Successfully* and *Why Be Afraid?*

Overcoming Common Problems

HOW TO LOVE AND BE LOVED

Dr Paul Hauck

SHELDON PRESS
LONDON

First published in Great Britain in 1983 by
Sheldon Press, SPCK, Marylebone Road, London NW1 4DU

Third impression 1989

First published in the USA in 1983 by
The Westminster Press, Philadelphia, Pennsylvania

British Library Cataloguing in Publication Data

Hauck, Paul
    How to love and be loved.—(Overcoming common
    problems)
    1. Interpersonal relations
    I. Title   II. Series
    158′2   HM132

    ISBN 0-85969-394-5

Typeset by Inforum Ltd, Portsmouth
Printed in Great Britain by
Richard Clay Ltd, Bungay, Suffolk

Jacqueline Hauck
and
Robert Fielding
I dedicate this book to you
for all the love you gave mom and pop

Contents

Preface

Do you want to love someone? And do you want someone to love you too? Of course you do. That's what most people want. Then why do so many people have trouble getting along with each other? What can you do to overcome these problems? And how can you establish and continue loving relationships?

This book will give you answers, and it can give you a better life. Here you can find out about the reciprocity theory of love, the business theory of marriage, and the 'love disorders' that cause so much trouble. You can learn the three rules for achieving co-operation, respect, and love and the four options available to you when you encounter frustration. You will also become acquainted with the thoughts that confuse your relationships — the twelve irrational ideas that you can overcome. You can even learn how to take the drastic steps that may be necessary as a last resort.

Most important, you will learn how to love and be loved.

1
The problem of love

It is one of the most desired conditions in the world. People seek it all of their lives but seldom get enough of it. It is a commodity for which people have an insatiable appetite. The more they get, the more they want. It creates feelings of the most intense delight such that, with its first encounter, people remember it forever. However, it is also one of the most painful conditions. People kill themselves and others over it. It is on the minds of the masses to such an extent that probably no other subject has been expressed in so much song, poetry, and prose.

Without it the infant dies. Without it the adult becomes emotionally misshapen. It is a powerful thing, but it is very unstable. Because of it we sometimes exhibit the very best within us, and sometimes it causes us to exhibit the very worst within us. In short, it is one of the most misunderstood subjects in the world.

What is it? Love, of course.

Throughout my years as a clinical psychologist in public and private practice I have come upon countless clients who had difficulties in their love lives and in their marriages. For many years I was at a loss as to how to understand many of these problems because I frankly had no philosophical framework by which to guide myself. As my experience increased, however, I gained insights into the mysteries of love and marriage and began theorizing and writing about them.

One of the insights I gained was that more people were disturbed over their love lives than any other single problem. They might come to me exhibiting such emotions as depression, anger, anxiety, jealousy, or excessive passivity; and sometimes these would be in connection with their careers, disciplining the children, or perhaps even financial matters. However, the single most frequent life situation which precipitated any of these emotions was clearly the troubled marriage or romance.

Love disorders

The subject of love is probably one of the most misunderstood subjects in the whole world. Here are examples that illustrate how unaware of the problems of love some intelligent, educated, and professional people can be.

Not very long ago I heard this piece of advice given on a television show. A doctor was advising a female patient whose marriage was in difficulty; after listening very patiently, he leaned over, put his hand on the patient's hand, patted it a few times and said with a loving smile, 'I think what your marriage needs Mary is to have another baby.' I used to think this was only soap opera stuff until I ran into my own clients who told me how often they received this advice from their friends, clergymen, or doctors. To me this clearly signifies that these advisors have little or no appreciation of what makes a marriage tick. In reality, that advice might well have been sensible for only the most minute percentage of the married population. The vast majority of married couples do not need another child when their marriage is in dificulty. To burden a woman with another child when she has serious difficulties with the other children or with her husband is pure insanity. If a man wants to leave a marriage because of the difficulty he is having with his wife and his children, or the financial burdens which he must wrestle with daily, the suggestion that he take on another child will only increase his frustrations and financial strain.

The fact that such ludicrous pieces of advice are given in all seriousness shows clearly that most of us haven't the foggiest notion as to what causes marital discord or how to solve it.

Just how unaware we are of the difficulties inherent in handling love and marriage sensibly is illustrated by the enormous difficulty we have when trying to decide on two of the most important questions that will ever confront us in a lifetime. The first one is 'At what age should I marry?', and the second one is, 'Whom should I marry?' Neither one of these questions has been answered by research in any definitive way. At the present time these matters are handled mostly by the heart, not by the head. And in spite of all the research that has gone on in the social sciences, little headway has been made in helping people know when and with whom to spend the rest of their lives. It has often been said, we can put a man on the moon but we can't cure the common cold. It also is true that we can put a man on the moon but we can't tell our young daughters or sons when the best time is for them to marry and with what kind of a person they would be happiest.

It seems to me that it is high time people became aware of just where love is located with respect to the major human motivations. Is love the greatest of our drives and motives, or is it among our weakest? It turns out that love is at about the mid-point between the most basic and the highest motivations.

Abraham Maslow, a psychologist who formulated a theory of motivation, suggested that we are all driven by five motives. The most basic motivations are the strongest and when they have been reasonably satisfied we develop interest in the next set of motivations and so on up the pyramid until we come to the fifth level of motivation. In their rank of importance they are as follows:

1 Physiological needs
2 Safety needs
3 Belongingness and love needs
4 Esteem needs
5 Self-actualization needs

We cannot of course dispute the fact that physiological needs are the most basic. When a person is hungry, cold, or thirsty, nothing else in the world matters except food, clothing, or water. All of us feel better if, once the body has been fed and watered, we have a place that will protect us from the elements and the danger around us.

Next come the needs of belonging and love. And why not? After all, the inside of the body is now well taken care of, and the environment is reasonably controlled, so it is time for us to bring in another human being with whom we can associate intimately. People want to have affection from others, to have companionship, to ward off loneliness, and to be able to satisfy sexual appetites as well.

Note carefully however, this need for belonging and love ranks third in the list, not first as many people seem to think. Judging by everyday behaviour, we would gain the impression that the only thing people are interested in is love, love, and more love. Actually this is the impression we get only because we have our physiological and our safety needs so satisfied that most of us don't give them a second thought. If suddenly our food supply were endangered or a tornado tore the house off its foundation, however, I can assure you we would not think about going to a dance tonight. We would be worried about whether or not we had a roof over our heads.

Needs for esteem gain importance next, after we feel we have been loved and are acceptable human beings to others. It is at this time that we want to strive for achievement, to demonstrate adequacy, to show the world that we are competent and that we can be independent and free. This is also the time in our lives when we want to have prestige, recognition, and attention for our efforts.

The last needs on the list are the needs for self-actualization. These are our desires to become all that we are capable of becoming. Self-actualization is the total and complete fulfilment of your inner destiny.

When we look at these five needs we can perhaps begin to appreciate a bit more the vital, but not pre-eminent, place that love has in the scheme of things. Needing love is a temporary phase in our growth which leads us on to yet higher motivations such as self-esteem and self-actualization. Let us, therefore, always consider the drive for love and acceptance as not the strongest nor the weakest of motivations. It is a prerequisite for the higher motivations and can be reduced in importance once it has served its purpose of lifting us up to the fourth and fifth levels. Just as we do not concern ourselves with finding food to survive each day, so we do not look about us every day for proof of our worth (by being loved and approved of by people) once we have passed that stage.

The last point I wish to make which may prove to you how truly unaware we are of love as a human condition is that it has never become a designation in psychological diagnosis. I think it could be.

What name would you give to the condition of someone who is intelligent, well-adjusted, handsome or beautiful, but who suddenly becomes depressed, tearful, insanely jealous, and is perhaps ready to commit suicide? Either we have all gone through such periods of temporary disturbance or we know of people who have been through them. We all know someone who has been so madly in love that he or she was willing to lay down his life for the woman of his dreams or her life for the man who has fulfilled her fantasies! When a football star of the high school comes to therapy, ready to die because his girl friend has broken up with him, are we dealing with a simple case of depression? Are we dealing with a transient adolescent disorder? Are we dealing with a longstanding and ineffective personality problem? I think not. We are dealing with a condition which I have called 'Love Disorder'.

Love Disorder is a very painful or exhilarating condition similar to manic-depressive psychosis. It has the same capability as a psychosis of making you feel as though you were flying on wings of song or sitting in a dungeon. This is a condition that afflicts young and old. And the first time it hits, it is sometimes the most deadly. In any event, it causes us to lose our reason, to forget every other important thing that our lives are concerned with, to forget food, drink, sleep, and work. If that isn't a neurotic reaction, what is?

Being in love can cause us to behave foolishly and fill us with pain. It is not a laughing matter when you see a person actually suffering the intense agonies of an unfulfilled love desire. These people suffer in unique ways, and they suffer intensely. It is not enough to teach them to stop blaming themselves so that their depressions end. What is required for lasting health is for them to fall *out* of love. Falling in or out of love is like going in and out of debt. The first step is easy, the second is anything but.

Causes of the problem

In understanding the reasons why loving couples quarrel and eventually fall out of love, I do not intend to go down a long list of obvious facts about why people don't get along. Rather, I want to give you insights into what I have found from many years of counselling people with marriage problems.

If I were asked to identify the most common underlying failure that men and women have in a marriage or a relationship that has become inefficient, self-defeating, and highly stressful, I would have to say it is the failure to realize how important it is for them to maintain a reasonable degree of satisfaction in their relationship. Too many of you have been taught throughout the years that the best way to get someone to love you is to give in to the other person endlessly and that the more you give, the more love will be returned to you.

This statement needs to be qualified. If it means that you are having your own needs and desires satisfied at the same time, then well and good. However, if you are constantly sacrificing without reciprocity, the marriage or the relationship will almost certainly be in serious trouble. It is my observation that being *very* passive, loving, and giving, creates stress. One of the best remedies for this is to learn how to become assertive. In brief, I have found that one of the best cures for a bad marriage is to teach one of the parties involved, and sometimes both of them, how to get *more* benefits from the marriage. Most unhappiness in marriages and relationships occurs because one or both persons have sacrificed too much. Being thoughtless about your own desires and needs is ultimately not only bad for you but bad for the children and partner.

The woman in particular has been taught to be submissive to the man and to put all of the male's concerns over her own. This has had the effect of making her submissive to his interests, and automatically creates antagonism in the woman towards her husband. This is best illustrated when a couple are making love. If the female focuses constantly on whether her lover is enjoying himself, she will, in all likelihood, not be able to achieve sexual pleasure herself. If she is willing to focus on her own sexual pleasures and also to focus on his, that could work quite well.

A person who is obsessively concerned about another's welfare develops problems of possessiveness and jealousy. Instead of allowing each other the freedom that goes a long way towards enhancing the feelings of love, they tend to smother and stifle those wonderful feelings for one another. Too many adolescents have been told that the more we love someone the more we will be loved. That sounds beautiful and mature and, if carried off properly, is in fact a workable ideal. Unfortunately, it is an idea which easily becomes perverted and turns into a series of one-sided interactions between a giver and taker. Any relationship that becomes unbalanced, with one partner giving a great deal and the other receiving a great deal, will simply end up being a sick relationship. We must base our marriage or relationship conduct, not on total sacrifice for the other person, but on reciprocal sacrifice. This is a mature and healthy approach rather than a selfish one. And it should be free of guilt.

Regarding the balance between how much one person has to give as contrasted with what another one expects, the important consideration is not how much you are giving to your partner, but rather how much you value what you are getting.

One of my male clients told me once that he had a very happy marriage because his wife gave him everything he expected. I was rather surprised at this remark because I always had thought of him as being someone who had been denied a great deal. His wife appeared to a number of my associates as a rather indulged person. He maintained, however, that all he wanted from her was to stay home and take care of the children, to keep a nice home, and to be faithful to him. For these benefits, he was willing to exchange practically anything she asked for. She controlled the family finances, could stay out late, buy clothes and jewellery, and even go on holiday with her relatives or girlfriends. He got what he wanted and was quite content.

People who differ vastly in certain important ways don't stand a ghost of a chance of being happy with one another. How could they be? After all, we tend to be comfortable with people who are somewhat like us, who think like us, who enjoy the same kinds of recreational activities, food, political views, and so on. It is, therefore, extremely important when falling in love to analyse your degree of compatibility.

There are essentially two kinds of incompatibility: neurotic and profound. Neurotic incompatibility is that which exists between two people who are basically well suited to each other but who, because of temporary emotional difficulties, are not getting along well. Clear up the emotional problems and things go along smoothly. As a matter of fact, most of the people who come for counselling are precisely of this type.

Profound incompatibility, on the other hand, stems from differences between the partners so great that a peaceful coexistence between them is almost unthinkable. For example, a very religious person is almost bound to be extremely unhappy living with an atheist. One of my female clients was very much in love with a man and wanted to marry him but, because he was not a Christian, she simply could not entertain the thought of ever living with him. That was a profound incompatibility and I agreed with her decision completely.

Other forms of profound incompatibility have to do with such issues as whether disciplining the children should be firm or lax, whether money should be spent or saved, or whether sex should happen twice a day or twice a month. These incompatibilities are so very fundamental to the values which each of us treasure, that to have them in our own homes is more than a frustrating experience, it is a *profoundly* frustrating experience.

One of the major reasons for these differences in the way two people approach problems is their upbringing. Family backgrounds are much more important in determining how a person deals with issues and adopts philosophies than is generally appreciated. There are a great many people who see me who have difficulties in their marriages precisely because they did not take the cultural and social background of their partners into consideration when they married them. One woman, for example, was surprised that her husband lacked ambition, spent hours in front of the television, seldom helped around the house with the children or the dishes, and would routinely take off with his friends on fishing or hunting trips. Yet, when I explored the background he came from, it turned out that his father was very much like this; and his mother always tolerated it. So in effect, she married a man who was raised in a home where a father went to work, returned home, rested up, and had his social life separate from his wife's. So why shouldn't this woman's husband be the way he was raised? Had she paid the slightest bit of attention to the home from which her husband came, she would have been able to predict fairly accurately what her own husband would be like.

One of the strongest pieces of advice I have for people who are engaged is to spend as much time with your future in-laws as you possibly can. Observe how they treat each other, what their political and religious views are, how they deal with money, and whether they quarrel or calmly talk things out. Do not make the naïve assumption that your future husband or your future wife will be vastly different from what you are looking at in his or her family. People behave as they are raised. They can change, I agree. However, those changes are usually some years ahead. You can rest assured that the philosophies, the temperament, and the lifestyle with which your lover was raised are going to be an integral part of the relationship you will have for a good many years to come.

Another poorly understood fact that causes friction in otherwise healthy relationships is the tendency on the part of people to undergo normal and repeated changes throughout the years. The person you married when you were in your early twenties will not be the same person when you are thirty. A young man may be interested in riding motorcycles, in getting drunk with the boys, and wanting to play more than work when he is around twenty. When he is about thirty years old he may give up motorcycles for economy cars, he may change his friends from the rowdy bunch to the more business minded or intellectual kind, and he may simply settle down in other ways which would have been considered boring and unthinkable when he was a younger man. And of course, the same applies to women. They may undergo changes from being passive and dependent on their husbands for decisions and for support. As they grow older they become less fearful, more independent, and more grown up; and their husbands may not enjoy living with these changes.

I find that people change fairly regularly about every seven to ten years. I recognize that these are very imprecise figures. Whether changes come every five, seven, or ten years is not as important, however, as is the fact that you can depend upon people changing. This is one of the reasons that divorces happen even after many years of marriage. It merely signifies that enough time has passed and enough changes and growth have taken place in one or both lovers that the things that made him or her happy at one time are no longer able to do so. We are, after all, changeable human beings. It should come as no surprise, therefore, that we usually want different things as we go through life.

A marvellous thing often happens to people when they reach the age of thirty or the ages between twenty-eight and thirty-two. It is in this age span that many people for the first time are able to understand what life is all about. They can look back over the previous years and understand them in an entirely new way. They can get insights into their own behaviour that were totally inaccessible to them before. It is as though they have been walking uphill through a dense forest and finally reached a clearing and are able to look back and see where they have been. For many that's what it's like to be thirty years old.

The psychological and practical meaning of becoming thirty is that this is often a stressful period for marriage. The person who has just attained that age may begin to change in very healthy ways, and this can sometimes be of great annoyance to the partner who may not like these changes. Men, for example, will often become more assertive, more goal-directed, and in general act more maturely. Women frequently become less dependent, thus less co-operative, and in general become less fearful. To an insecure man this obviously presents serious problems. If he has not profited greatly by attaining the age of thirty and his wife has, then we have a pronounced imbalance in terms of maturity. If she becomes very mature at this point in her life and he does not, then she will think that she has a child for a husband instead of a man.

A further cause for many frictions between partners is that they do not realize that maintaining a marriage is simply one of the most difficult of all normal human endeavours. Marriage requires dedication, patience, and the acceptance of long-range responsibilities that are often crushing in their intensity. A young woman who had been married for only two years made the point to me that marriage is stifling, demanding, inhibiting, and often difficult. Yet she did not want a divorce; she was very happily married. I feel she had an entirely correct understanding of her situation. Those starry-eyed, naïve, and romantically dazed youngsters who think that being married is going to be a perpetual holiday are doomed to a rude awakening. When they are unable to pay bills, or one ignores the other unfairly, or he no longer has his freedoms because he has a family he must work for, or she finds herself confined at home because she has two babies who need constant attention, then for the first time will they begin to realize the true meaning of marriage and its heavy commitments.

I want to make it absolutely clear in this book that I think marriage is a wonderful and beautiful institution. It is one of the most rewarding of all human activities when successfully performed, and I urge most people to attempt it as a way of achieving long-term happiness.

Another impediment to marital and relationship harmony comes from the lack of appreciation we have for the very subtle but profound differences between men and women. Leaving the obvious physical differences aside it is positively fascinating, and a little bit strange, to note how frequently women from different backgrounds will come to counselling and all of them will make similar complaints. This consistency of viewpoint has convinced me that there are certain innate differences between men and women, not just differences in the way we bring up our little boys and girls.

When a boy, for example, becomes a man it is not very difficult for him to separate love from sex. He can have an argument with his wife or girlfriend one moment and want to take her to bed the next. In short, he can think of having sex with a woman and not care in particular about her as an individual. Men frequently make complaints of not getting enough sex from their wives and that they are being too possessed by women. Men often feel that they demonstrate their love for women by working hard for them, not getting drunk, coming home on time, and being faithful to them. They do not see why it is at all necessary to say 'I love you.' What are words compared to actions?

Women, on the other hand, far more often talk about wanting affection and love and do not mention sex at all. It is not as though they do not like sex, but love and affection embrace sex.

It is as though these qualities— love and sex— are inseparable. It is very difficult for them, therefore, to engage in sexual behaviour without having a great deal of fondness for their lover. To engage in sex casually is meaningless for them.

Another common characteristic among women is that they like to talk about how they feel, and they want to know how their lovers feel. The communication of feelings is for them an absolute requisite for sexual satisfaction. Not to know who she is sleeping with amounts to prostitution. If she cannot know what is going on in the heart of her mate, she will not want him as a mate. Deep feelings, therefore, and the communication of these feelings are more important than holding hands, buying a new dress, or taking a trip. Unless she has someone to whom she can bare her soul as well as her breast she is often not interested in him. That is a fact of feminine psychology a great many men do not understand, do not appreciate, and often do not like.

Women want to express themselves. They enjoy the release of feelings and intimacies, and they want to know exactly where they stand with those with whom they have a relationship. Men, on the other hand, do not need to know the inner recesses of the minds of their wives or girlfriends. And when they are troubled they often don't even want to communicate their troubles to their mates because they feel they should work out things by themselves. Women, however, often say that if they cannot talk about their problems they'll 'go crazy'. It makes a difference to whom they spill their troubles. It must be someone whom they respect and who has a sensitive ear and a soft shoulder. A man often doesn't care for such things, and he takes much more comfort in being able to deal with a problem himself.

A phenomenon, which I call 'catching-up', further illustrates the inability, in some instances, for a marriage to resolve its difficulties. Catching-up happens when a young man or woman marries too early and misses out on a lot of the fun that he or she might have had if the marriage had taken place years later. But since it did not, there comes a point in the lives of these people, perhaps at around thirty, sometimes at around forty, when the man or the woman wants to have freedom, to have other partners, or to get on a motorcycle and drive cross-country in a burst of adolescent excitement, simply because it is something that he or she never experienced.

If a man feels cheated because he married early and never had a fling, he must either learn to accept that fact and live with it gracefully, or he will have to put his marriage in great danger.

What partners say to each other in the heat of a fight and under the influence of great anger has a great deal to do with the future course of that relationship or marriage. My suggestion to all married couples is to keep your angry mouths shut. If you don't know how to control your anger then learn how. Do not shoot your mouth off in the heat of a battle just because you want to hurt your partner. You will regret this practice because you will lose points every time it happens. The day will arrive when there is no longer any feeling between the two of you. Eventually your mate will say, 'Okay, if you feel that way, I'll go. You'll get your divorce. You finally convinced me this was all a mistake.'

There are two further causes of marriage problems. The first has to do with the irrational notion: when people marry, they 'belong' to each other. People get the idea that to marry someone is to have acquired a piece of property. When they say 'you're mine' they aren't always using poetic or romantic language. They are using legal language. They mean: 'you are mine, you will do as I say, you cannot go where I don't allow, you cannot talk to whom I disapprove of', and so on and so forth.

Those people who never take this property idea seriously fare much better in a marriage. They know that a marriage is an agreement and that it may be a *temporary* agreement between two people who have accepted the understanding that they have a contract only as long as the arrangement works to a reasonable degree for both of them. They fully understand that, when an arrangement is no longer satisfying enough, either individual has a right to end the relationship and that it is sensible to do so.

Unfortunately, those who are insecure, who feel inferior, and who are super-sensitive about their own self-worth, often do think of their husbands or wives as property. They don't agree that people have the right to end the relationship. They believe that having a ring on the finger is equivalent to having a ring through the nose. And these are dangerous people. Often they are jealous, vicious, and angry to a psychotic degree.

The last cause of friction in marriages that I want to discuss is the need to be loved. People will simply sit and look aghast at me, with mouths open, when I point out to them that love is not necessary in life. It is as though I have said something blasphemous. One of our sacred loyalties is the enshrinement of love itself. He who does not regard love as the highest spiritual goal is thought of as being an animal. He who does not make love a second god is an unfeeling robot. It is claimed everyone must have love and that life is unbearable and horrible without it. Rejection is the greatest of insults and the worst danger a human being can face. Only in the love and approval of other people can we measure own value. Such is the importance given to the whole concept.

I take exception to this. Unless we are talking about helpless children I do not see how we can correctly claim that love is absolutely indispensable and that we are going to go into a life worse than hell if we are not loved by someone, intimately, and constantly.

The neurotic *need* for love rather than the practical *desire* for love, has caused more pain in people who are supposed to love each other than any other single thing.

Why do you have to be loved? Since when does somebody else's loving you make you a worthwhile human being? Weren't you worthwhile before you were loved? Will you let other people pass judgement on you (through their love) to say that you are worthwhile or not? There has to be something wrong when you turn such an evaluation over to other people who have no expertise concerning you. Why should any other person be able to tell you whether or not you are acceptable?

Think these things over very carefully. Ask yourself again and again whether or not the love of other people is really *critical* in your life rather than very *desirable*. Isn't being without love inconvenient, regrettable, and sad? Of course it is. But is it also horrible, terrible, tragic and the end of the world? If you think so, prove it!

Do not be misled by this last point. I am in no way against the deep feelings people develop for each other. I think they are positively wonderful, and I urge people to work very hard towards developing intimate relationships with those they care for. Life is so much nicer when those we care for care for us. But I do take exception to the idea that one *has* to have love constantly from that one particular person.

If you understand this point then you will forever be protected against the greatest fear people have: rejection. Rejection is to most people like a dagger in the heart. To be rejected by people we desire is to many of us the ultimate proof of how absolutely worthless we are. If we had worth we would never have been rejected.

But rejection is painless, *unless you make it hurt.* If you insist that you have turned into a nobody because your lover has rejected you, then you never had much of an ego to begin with. If you think that your life is over because your husband has found an interest in someone else, then you never had much confidence in yourself. If you think that because your lover is not talking to you the end of the world has come, you obviously have very few coping resources. In other words, the reaction to rejection, if it is a severe one, is simply a reflection of your own inadequacy and inferiority. You have been taught to believe in the bogey man. You have been taught to believe in ghosts, superstitions, in witches, in leprechauns, and in Easter bunnies. That's how much sense it makes to say that you, a well-functioning and intelligent adult, need the love of another person. I want to remind you how often you have broken up with loved ones already. Yet, when your other relationships dissolved you were able to survive them time after time and were able to find other people to relate to. Despite these repeated experiences you may still be repeating the same falsehoods to yourself: it is horrible to be rejected, I am going to die, it proves I am worthless, etc., etc.

Enough of this already! Let us grow up. Let us give ourselves credit for all the struggles we have gone through in life and consider rejection as just another frustration. Let us see ourselves as capable of recovery from these annoyances. Let us give ourselves credit for coping capacities which enable us to adjust to new societies, new countries, new jobs, new families, and the whole growth process itself. We are not children. We are adults. We are strong. We are capable. And we are desirable to many people in the world even though perhaps not by our present partners. So be it. Life will go on and our lives along with it.

The solution

The following chapters will describe three separate approaches that can succeed in getting you to love people and be loved in return. I first came across two of these approaches through the work of the psychologists, Charles and Clifford Madsen. The third approach comes from religious tradition.

The very simple points made by the Madsens were that they wanted to teach children that (1) when they did nice things, nice things happened to them, (2) when they did bad things, bad things happened to them. They further pointed out that these two simple principles were often disregarded and children were taught to expect entirely different consequences. The consequences they actually expected were: (*a*) when children did bad things, nice things sometimes happened to them; (*b*) when they did nice things, bad things were likely to happen; (*c*) it did not matter what a child did, bad things happened; and (*d*) it made no differences what a child did, nice things happened.

Let us return to the Madsens' first two principles, which seem to me to be very sensible but incomplete conceptualizations of what actually happens between two people. I would like to add a middle step and thereby formulate three rules for achieving co-operation, respect, and love.

Rule 1. If people treat you nicely, treat them nicely.
Rule 2. If people treat you badly, continue to treat them nicely, turn the other cheek, go the extra mile, and love those who trespass against you, *for a reasonable period of time*.
Rule 3. If people treat you badly, and *the second principle does not work*, treat them badly with approximately equal intensity, and without anger.

The beauty of this conceptualization is that it is based on scientific understanding and it is simplicity itself. I do not want to mislead you into thinking that it will therefore be easy. You will find that achieving co-operation, respect, and love with any of these three methods is going to be hard work indeed. But you will find at least that the world is not confusing, and that you can keep your sights on the goal through all kinds of subtle complexities. As long as you know where you are going and why, even if you have only a general conception of what you should be achieving, then any number of elements can enter into the picture and you will always know what your response to other people's behaviour can be.

Before we can delve into that, however, it is extremely important that you have a clear picture of what love actually is, and how, and why, marriage and loving relationships work.

2

The truth about love and marriage

The reciprocity theory of love

Love is that powerful feeling one has for persons, animals or things that has satisfied, is satisfying, or will satisfy our deepest desires and needs. This may not sound like a very original statement, but I assure you that a closer examination of it reveals a great many insights not easy to accept.

For example, the definition clearly indicates that it is not people that we love, it is rather what the people or animals or things do for us that we love. If the person you love does not satisfy you in ways that are extremely important to you, it is my belief that you simply fall out of love with him or her. If there are no satisfactions, benefits, or pleasures from that person, the love dies. The contrary is also true. The more someone satisfies your deep desires and needs the more you will be tempted to love that individual. But bear in mind again, it is not technically the individual you love, it is *what the person does for you*. Once you understand and accept that simple fact you will find it a great deal easier to create in others a feeling of love for you. You had better be a realist in this or you will not succeed. But once you accept reality and understand the nature of the true meaning of love, you will not fight your inclinations to give your partner what it takes for that partner to love you.

For example, if your partner wants you to have hygienic habits, then the more fastidious you are in your dress and in the care of your body, the more that person will love you. If it is also important for your partner to have much affection, then obviously the more you satisfy your partner's affectional needs by touching, holding hands, sitting side by side, and giving a warm embrace spontaneously, the more that person will love you.

And what about physical appearance, money, earning capacity and lifestyle? Do we also love people because they are rich, they dance well, or they are honest? That depends upon the values of the person making the judgements. If certain qualities are important to you, then you will naturally fall in love with people who have those qualities. Other people may have all kinds of other wonderful characteristics but they will simply not interest you because those are not important qualities in your particular case. This means that if financial security is important to you, or a rich lifestyle is one of your dreams, then you will naturally fall in love with someone who has wealth.

You may protest that this is not a demonstration of love, but only a deep caring about money. In other words, you might claim that it is not the person you care about, it is the person's money. If this is what you are thinking then you have failed to understand the point I made initially. One does not care for people unconditionally, one cares for what people do for us. If money is important to you, then it is not only the person you love, it is the money the person has, and the willingness on the part of that person to share it in your behalf. So money can become as legitimate a reason for loving someone as physical appearance, neatness, good sexual performance or any other piece of behaviour that happens to be valued by you.

But what if the financial security begins to diminish? Could a recession wipe out feelings of love in a family? You bet it could. Feelings of love can go down just as fast as the money in the bank does. And that's the way it is with all of the desires you have. The more they are satisfied, the more you are in love. The less they are satisfied, the less you feel in love. If you want a husband who is strong, makes decisions, will defend you against his family, and he does not do this, I can assure you that your feelings for him will diminish in direct proportion to the number of times he disappoints you. And if you, sir, value a woman who has a lovely figure and your wife begins to put on pound after pound, I can assure you too that your feelings of love will begin to fade as her pounds begin to mount.

I know this is anything but romantic in nature, but it is realistic. This is the way people are, like it or not. You may protest that people certainly aren't always loving others just because they are being treated kindly at the time. Surely there must be many examples when we love others and expect nothing in return. I disagree, but you must understand that I am talking about *intimate love,* not *fraternal love*. Intimate love has to do with one's partner, parents, children, relatives, or close friends. These are the people who affect us in our daily lives and for whom we are willing to make enormous sacrifices. When I am talking about my theory of love I am talking about the normal reciprocal process that always takes place among *intimate people*.

Fraternal love, or love of humankind, is a very noble human

sentiment also, but it does not require a similar expression of love in return. You may have been one of those generous persons who sent a package overseas to destitute families in a devastated country. You probably simply gave your cheque to the organization and hoped that it would bring good fortune to someone thousands of miles away. You did not care particularly who that person was, you did not expect an actual expression of thanks through the post or telephone, or in any other way. You did a good deed and you were happy in your heart that you were able to have enough good fortune to share this with someone else. The reward was knowing you had reduced someone else's suffering. That is non-intimate love, the love one has for one's fellow human being. It does not require 'giving' in return. In a sense it is, therefore, more noble than intimate love, which sooner or later does require payment for effort made. However, this is not totally accurate, either. Fraternal love works as it does because we are only occasionally asked to make sacrifices for people we don't know. It doesn't matter, therefore, whether they pay us back or not. But if they were to need us on a continual or almost daily basis I can assure you we would not regard them as distant people whom we want to please, but as very important people in our lives from whom we want to have some payment in return. That is one of the essential differences between intimate love and fraternal love. The former involves constant contact with people who are dear to us while the latter involves practically no contact. The former involves frequent sacrificing for one's loved ones while the latter calls for a mild and infrequent sacrifice. Therefore, I stick to my point that when it comes to an intimate relationship in your life, you will give to the other person as often as you feel comfortable and as long as you feel that you are getting a reasonable amount of satisfaction in return.

But what about our parents who are now aged, retired, or senile, and who can no longer pay us back for all the efforts and expense we are putting out to care for them? If you will recall my definition of love, I said that it was a feeling that we have for people who *did* (in the past), are (in the present), or *will* (in the future) satisfy our deepest desires and needs.

When we think back on all the wonderful efforts our parents made on our behalf but are not able to continue now because of old age, we can pay them back for the lifetime of sacrifice they made for us when we were younger. It is still reciprocating and paying off our indebtedness to them because we love them so dearly for the many efforts they made for us earlier.

But what about your children? What can a child do for you that would make you love the child? Surely the amount of benefit a child receives from a parent is enormously greater than the benefits the parent receives from the child. If the reciprocal theory of love holds true, how do we explain the great love that a parent has for a child?

Our benefits come in several ways: first, children do please us enormously and satisfy our deepest desires and needs by (a) proving that we can become parents, (b) perpetuating our own species, (c) carrying on the family name, and (d) often proving to be absolutely delightful, wonderful little creatures who bring great joy to our lives despite periodic disturbances.

Implications of the reciprocity theory of love

If you are following my thinking thus far and I am still making sense to you, then let us look at some further conclusions we can draw. You will see, I think, that there are some fascinating observations which come from accepting the basic premisses of the theory. I warned you before that the theory looks harmless but when you pursue the significance of these observations to their logical conclusions, the results can be surprising.

First, the theory sheds light on such questions as whether or not there is puppy love, whether infatuation is a distinct condition different from love, and whether love at first sight has any basis in fact.

When we use the expression 'puppy love', we generally refer to the strong feelings children have for one another or perhaps for an adult. The use of the word 'puppy' implies that this love is not a very serious one; it is cute, but it is not long-lasting, not deep, and is based only on the flimsiest considerations. And whatever else a person may say about it, the common thinking has it that puppy love is certainly not 'true' love.

I take complete exception to this view. Puppy love is a powerful emotion which arises out of the expectations and experiences of one person with another. Puppy love can be exquisitely deep, sincere, and just as painful when it breaks up as any adult romance. The worst you can say about this situation is that the child is being foolish, impractical, and blind. But you cannot say that he or she is not in love.

Infatuation is the usual term applied when two adults love each other superficially and fleetingly. I think we do such persons a serious disservice when we don't take their experience seriously and do not recognize it as a very powerful love feeling. A couple who have been married happily for fifty years love each other for similar reasons as do two people who have fallen in love rapidly and who may be blinded by their passions. For those who have just started a passionate relationship the claim that they are in love is validated in the same way it is for us all, namely, that they are convinced the other person will satisfy his or her deepest desires and needs. The fact that they may be wrong is only sad. It does not alter their feelings that they are now on the verge of a beautiful existence with another person.

We supposedly run into cases of infatuation where middle-aged adults suddenly fall in love with the strangest partners. The forty-year-old male who suddenly wants to run off with a younger woman with several children but can find no fault with his own wife or family is, in the minds of some people, suffering from infatuation. If by infatuation we mean he was unwise in his behaviour for overreacting to a tender relationship, and that he cannot see the forest for the trees, then I would agree that he is suffering from infatuation. However, to claim he does not have very powerful feelings for the other woman is to deny what all love feelings are like. If we are going to label as infatuations all middle-age love relationships not based on rational considerations, then we had better refer to 95 per cent of all marriages as infatuations! Most of them were initiated at a younger age when there was much less rational control.

'Love at first sight' is a special class of infatuation. It is a powerful feeling which sometimes strikes an individual not even having been introduced to the object of affection. When you see a stranger across a crowded room and you fall in love at long range, you are obviously the world's champion risk taker. You are concluding, with only the flimsiest of evidence, that the person across the room has the capacity to make you a happy human being. Perhaps he or she moves right, laughs right, dresses right, looks good; and on those pleasant but not terribly significant considerations you are making a prediction about what that person can do for you.

This love-at-first-sight phenomenon is every bit as genuine, sincere, and valid a love experience as is puppy love, infatuation, based on an expectation that one's deepest desires and needs can be fulfilled by that other person. Sometimes these hunches work out amazingly well. Sometimes they are complete fiascos. I suspect the latter result happens more often than the former.

Another insight which arises out of the reciprocity theory of love is that you have every right in the world to expect your mate to change in any way that it takes to satisfy your deepest desires and needs. Though you might have married a partner with a set of habits that pleased you five years ago, do not apologize at this point for saying that you do not like these habits anymore and that some of them have to change. To suggest that we should not request changes in our mates is simply nonsense. If behaviour exists that we don't like, are we supposed to accept it graciously? Are we such fools that we think we must live without complaining about a situation that brings us misery? When you are questioned with that age old statement 'Why can't you accept me as I am?', you had better respond, 'Because I don't like you that way. It makes me unhappy when you do those things. I didn't mind those things years ago but I've changed and I don't want to tolerate that behaviour anymore.'

And why shouldn't you change? As I tried to show in Chapter one, we never stay the same, we are always different people from day to day, and from one year to the next. Anyone who believes the world stands still, or that people remain the same as when they met just isn't functioning with all his or her faculties. Expecting new things from each other is as natural as women loving diamonds and men loving meat and potatoes. This seems to me to be such an obvious fact that I marvel when I hear some of my clients apologize for the pressures they want to put upon their mates.

If you agree with my definition of love, then you can easily see my next point: love must generally be earned. Only in the cases of infants, pets, and senile parents does love not need to be earned. In most other instances that feeling which we designate as love emerges from us *after* we have been gratified. It is something which evolves out of the other person's behaviour. Not that it is directly caused by the other person, but it is a feeling we allow ourselves to have after someone has proven to us that we are extremely important to them. Then we permit their behaviour to have a very positive effect on us.

That is why it is *incorrect* to ask people to give you love. What you really are asking for is certain behaviours which please you enormously and that cause you to love the giver. You don't *get* love, you create it inside yourself *after* your deep desires and needs are met. It is the action that they give us, and it is the feeling that we experience. The person receiving gratification of desires and needs creates his or her own feeling of love over your kindness.

The next implication from the reciprocity theory is that love means different things to different people. Just as one man's meat is another man's poison, so too, what is a loving act to one person is not necessarily a loving act towards another person. When you want someone to love you it is extremely important that you try to understand what it takes to make that person happy. You had better not interpret happiness just as you see it, but also consider how the other person defines happiness. A typical example of confusion of desires and expectations arises in the giving of flowers as a sentimental gesture. Men often rebel at the practice of giving women flowers to show their love. And from my point of view, being a man, I can understand completely their rational, brilliant, correct, and practical thinking. Wanting flowers to prove one's love is obviously ridiculous because the flowers die in a few days, they are rather expensive, and they require no effort on the part of the person aside from spending money to acquire them. The man who is faithful to his wife, works hard to support her and the family, and permits her the same freedoms that he enjoys, is showing her a hundred times more affectionate and loving behaviour than three dozen long stem roses could ever show. At least that is the male argument.

But we are now not talking about what it takes to make the man love her, we are asking what it takes to make her love him. And if she says it's long stem roses, then it's long stem roses! She may be foolish in this regard. She may be adolescent, romantic, impractical, and a victim to too many Gothic novels. That's totally irrelevant. If she wants flowers to prove your love, that's what you had better realize and that's what you had better give.

It should by now be obvious that one of the most logical conclusions that emerges from the above discussion is that for adults, love must be earned. We may all be able to love our cute french poodles and our parakeets without conditions but this simply does not apply to adults from whom we expect to satisfy a certain number of desires and needs. This perhaps comes as a very unflattering discovery about human nature.

The notion of having to earn a person's love is actually not a foreign idea to mature persons. Without being told, they usually appreciate the fact that one has to reciprocate in interpersonal relationships in order to make the relationship work. If you are a spoiled or immature person then it hardly occurs to you that you owe people for their efforts on your behalf. Stop believing you have a right to expect love, justice, a job, security, and so on. If you get them that's wonderful, but you may be just plain lucky. The idea of paying your mate back for every effort he or she makes is simply very foreign to the immature person. You can use this observation as a way of determining very quickly if your partner is mature or not. If he or she is always raising the roof when you ask for a reasonable favour although you have knocked yourself out for him or her, then you have a child on your hands. People who (a) think things always have to go their way and (b) become bitter, angry, or resentful when things do not go their way, are by definition immature persons.

A frequent statement I hear from my clients, and which makes them feel either angry or guilty is, 'I hate it when my mate uses me.' Or, 'I feel very guilty when I think I am using my mate.' The idea that we use each other in a loving relationship seems to be so unacceptable and unflattering that people automatically want to deny it or stop doing what they are doing if they conclude that they are in fact being used or doing the using. And yet, is this not what is actually happening between all people who love each other? Of course we use each other. If I have desires and needs which I cannot satisfy by myself then I am obviously interested in a relationship with another human being because it is the other human being who can satisfy those desires and needs for me. So I am using that person's skills, interests, talents, financial resources, looks, or whatever I need, in order to make me a happier person. And the same goes in the other direction. You are being used because of certain advantages you can give the other person that will make that individual happier. There are very few relationships that are not somehow reciprocal in nature. The only time a relationship is not based on reciprocity is when one person is doing all the giving and getting nothing in return. If you help someone who is powerless to do you a favour, or pay you for your services, or to help you in any way at all, then that is a non-reciprocal relationship and is the one exception to the rule of our using each other. If you want to be a good Samaritan and pick up injured persons on the highway, take them to the nearest hospital, see to it that they are taken care of, and then drive off like the Lone Ranger without waiting for thanks or recognition, more power to you. Just being of service is apparently all the reward you need. But that again refers to the fraternal love I spoke of before. When a relationship becomes more intense and is based on very frequent contacts then we all become somewhat self-interested and do not want to give endlessly. We expect to receive as well. And that is what I have come to expect.

Let us stop feeling guilty over the fact that we use each other. Of course we do. I use my secretaries for their skills and my secretaries use me for the salary that they earn. I use my grocer because he gives me vegetables, and I give him dollars. We use our mates for a hundred different services, and they expect a hundred back. To suggest, therefore, that you are cheap and degraded because you are only staying with someone to use him or her is absurd.

The business theory of marriage

Marriages are made by two individuals who have made the judgement that they have a higher than average degree of compatibility and can please each other to such an extent that institutionalizing the relationship seems only logical. Why let a marvellous person in your life just float in and out when, with effort and commitment, that relationship could flower into a lifelong partnership? So rather than simply shake hands on the deal and flip a coin as to who will move in with whom, people, as civilization has become more complex, have created the institution of marriage. This makes the two lovers aware of the fact that they have committed themselves to each other, that they have certain legal obligations to each other that normally do not exist until they are married, and that this now has the backing and approval of society, one's personal friends, and the law courts themselves. It is a serious business because in most cases before many years pass it will involve other human beings and an estate, which, at times, can amount to a fortune. With all this at stake it only makes sense to legitimize the relationship.

For the woman in particular, it is a critical move. When she agrees to walk down the aisle with her fiancé and to make herself vulnerable to whatever good or bad fortune may come of her husband's efforts to provide for her during periods when she is rather helpless (either during periods of pregnancy, illness, or the rearing of a family), she had better have some guarantees that she will not be abandoned casually during these critical times. If she is going to allow herself to be in the position of giving birth and rearing children she will certainly want to have reassurance in some form that she will not starve, have to give the children away, or go into prostitution to support herself and the children. In this respect she is simply being intelligent, using good judgement, using her head rather than her heart, and facing the reality of what might happen to her if she does not make some hard business decisions.

A man owes a woman this kind of reassurance because, if the two of them want a family, it is so ordained that she will be the one who will carry the child, deliver it, and in most cases rear it. This means that she will have to forego many of her own career plans which, if she were not to raise a family for herself and her husband, would at times allow her to have a very interesting life and sometimes even allow her to acquire considerable wealth. But being a housewife and homemaker does not always coincide with being able to support oneself in a reasonable style. That is an unspoken agreement the couple make when they get married and decide to have a family. Therefore, she has as much right to his income as he had because she forfeited her opportunity for an independent wage when she decided to please them both by having a family. It is entirely unfair to a man to expect his wife to give him a family, to give up her own career, and then to insist that the money he makes is his when there is no other way he could have had a family. It surprises me how many women do not understand their rights to the husband's earnings because of that fact. I have talked to hundreds of women who do not know how much their husbands earn and who have no say in the purchase of the next car. They accept the fact that, because he actually did the work, the money is his and she must be content with his sense of generosity to let her have enough for a dress or groceries. This is chauvinism at its worst. And too many women abide by it.

A woman in this condition does not give herself the credit she deserves. She has every right to equal control over the family funds for two more reasons. The first is that she certainly earns every penny she shares with her husband because she services his needs and the family needs in dozens of ways. Most women don't sit at home throwing bon-bons in their mouths and getting fat while they watch TV all day. The average housewife works hard, handles a multitude of responsibilities, and often lives a lonely and boring life that would drive the husband nuts if he tried it for three days. Any husband who doesn't believe this ought to spend two weeks at home while his wife goes off on holiday. In a great many instances the man finds out just what it is like to care for children, pets, laundry, cooking, and keeping the house ship-shape just so she won't gripe when she comes home.

The next reason why women have a right to equal control over the funds is that they are the blue-collar workers of the family, and unless they strike once in a while their deep desires and needs will go completely ignored. Isn't it odd that the same man who walks the picket line against the factory that will not recognize his reasonable demands, will go home and take the role of management in his own house and strenuously reject offers from his wife which she makes in the role of labourer. It does seem as though what we regard as right or wrong depends largely on whether we are asking or giving.

However this may be, it is extremely important that you begin to look upon a marriage as a business arrangement between two people who had better get a fair amount of happiness from the business if they don't want it to collapse. A factory cannot succeed if either management or labour are not getting a fair share of the benefits, and a marriage cannot succeed if the same conditions are not met. Therefore, try to see the marriage as a business arrangement between one partner joining forces with another rather than as an employer and an employee. The marriage is like a company called Smith and Co.; and if the company makes a profit the marriage is happy. Happiness in marriage is the equivalent of a profit in a business. Being in the red, having more debts than you can pay for is, in marriage terms, being unhappy. The similarities between a business and a marriage go on. If you don't like your job, you quit it. In marriage that's called desertion. If you want to leave your job permanently, you resign or get fired. In a marriage that's called a divorce.

It is my observation that those marriages which spell out the conditions of the marriage beforehand often have less difficulty than those that do not do so. And aren't they acting like a couple of business people when they do this? If a man and a woman decide that they will put money away every month to buy a house, that they will have a family started no later than three years after the marriage, that they will alternate spending Christmas at each other's parental homes, and so on, this couple will usually encounter fewer frustrations than the couple which has made no such plans.

A marriage and a business handle frustrations in very similar manners. If an employer is unhappy with an employee he or she notifies the employee and makes a suggestion that the tardiness be corrected, that the employee spend less time on breaks away from the job, or that the work be done more carefully. In a marriage, husband and wife also have frequent conversations describing their mutual frustrations and how they would like to see them altered. He wants her to keep the house a bit cleaner. She wants him to be a little bit more giving of his time to the children.

If these similarities between business and marriage don't impress you, then what about the fact that both of them involve huge sums of money, they take legal means to organize the marriage or the company, and they require legal measures to end them. And need I remind you that for hundreds of years a marriage was not primarily a matter of love at all, but an agreement to cement governments, countries, or tribes. It was strictly a business arrangement in which cattle were offered or dowries were expected.

You don't like the idea that your marriage is a business arrangement? Frankly I don't like it either. When you take away all the hearts and flowers, you are left with a pretty hard-nosed business arrangement. And if you don't believe that, you should just hear some of my clients talk about how they are going to take the husband or wife to the cleaners once they get them into the court room. And what do you think they are going to fight over in court? Custody of the children, support payments, alimony, and how to divide up the furniture, the house, and the car. That's not a bingo game; it's hard finance.

The notion of marriage being a loving business may be harder to accept by men than by women. I have a hunch that women have always seen marriage as a business arrangement about which they had better be quite practical. That hasn't been the case with men. That's why I feel the male is by far the more romantic of the two. When he falls in love he actually does not regard the relationship as much a business as the female does. I am not praising him over the female when I say this, I am only making an observation.

For example, this is why men fall in love much more quickly than women. In considering his proposal to marry, the man usually thinks of sex, having a home and family. He likes her looks, he likes her figure, and she seems reasonably easy to get along with. What other considerations does the man *need* to think of when he makes a proposal? He usually isn't going to ask himself whether she can support him. At least that's not the way it's been for hundreds of years. He isn't going to ask himself if she would desert him if he becomes handicapped or pregnant. Young men don't think they can ever die, much less be incapacitated. In short, he doesn't want a lot *from* her. He wants *her*. He'll supply the rest for himself.

For the woman it is quite another matter. She is a fool if she does not think of the marriage in very practical and businesslike terms. Most parents accept this in regard to their daughters. If the girl brings home a young man in whom she is interested, what is the first thing we parents want to know about him? We of course want to know what he looks like, what he acts like, whether he's a man of character and intelligence or whether he's a knucklehead. And we certainly want to know what his educational background is, his work experience, the skills he has, and how responsible and hard working he is. Why do we ask those questions of the male much more than of the female? Because he is usually the one expected to bring home the money. He will earn the living while the woman will sooner or later have a family and have to stay home to care for the children. Even though there are women who do a better job of supporting their husbands than vice versa, or who are able to have a career and children at the same time, my statement is true on the average for most of the women throughout the world. They become dependent on the man's skill for bringing home the bread and the bacon. It is therefore incumbent upon them (and very wise besides), if they look him over very carefully, not just for his sex appeal, but for what kind of a father he is going to be, if he is going to be a considerate husband, whether he's going to be a drunk, and whether he is going to be able to provide her with the kind of living she enjoys. This is why the men who make the most money, who show the most promise, who have the best education, become the most eligible bachelors.

Think of two contests, one featuring the most desired bachelors in a city, and one featuring the most eligible single women. What are we thinking of when we think of each? Are we going to judge both by the same standards? Of course not. The most eligible bachelor is going to be someone who is loaded with dough, dripping with charm, dresses like a fashion plate, looks like a movie star but most of all can give a woman a lifestyle that she has always dreamed of. It's great of course if he happens to be as handsome as a movie star, but that isn't the biggest drawing card as far as women are concerned. If he's bald headed and not particularly good looking, but he's a charming man and he has great financial security, that will make up for what he lacks in physical appearance.

But the most eligible single woman has to have curves all in the right places, a lovely head of hair, white pearly teeth, look like a model for a beer advertisement, and then have the right personality and character. She doesn't have to have wealth. If she is packed solidly and enjoys being made love to she's practically won him over.

That's why I say it is the man who tends to be the romantic. His heart and soul are focused on the physical and social pleasures the woman can give him. Her focus is just as often on the material advantages she can get from him, along with what she feels for him personally. She is the practical one, the man is the dreamer.

A word of caution, and a word of defence. I am not criticizing women because of this statement. I accept it as reality, and I am not making a judgement about it. Nor am I saying that men always remain more romantic than the women. Actually, after the honeymoon, if often turns out that he loses much of his romanticism while she gains more. The tables are turned: she often winds up craving him on a personal level much more than he craves her, and he finally wants more material things and fun with others than he does with his wife.

Just after I had written the above remarks, I met my next client, a woman who was living with a man with whom she had just had an argument. She was dependent upon him financially; so it was quite a shock when he asked her to pack up her bags and leave his home. My client was capable of dealing with this sudden reversal and had some means by which she could survive the temporary hardship. However, she pointed out (without my asking) that she could now understand why women want to be brides rather than mistresses. As she put it, 'There is simply no protection for the woman if she breaks up with the fellow. At least if she's married, she has child support rights, she shares in his estate, insurance benefits, and perhaps alimony. At my age that makes a whale of a difference when a relationship ends as suddenly as mine just did.'

I wondered why she hadn't figured this out years ago since she was a perfectly intelligent woman. I had to conclude that she was basically one of those romantic types much like the men I've been describing. She lost the sense of practicality that most of her sisters have, and this experience made her realize again what love and marriage are truly all about.

Do you begin to understand why I called marriage a loving business? Is it still so difficult to see a marriage as an agreement similar to any other contract? Unless the terms of the contract are met, the relationship, no matter what kind it is, will be broken. I contend therefore that those marriages that are run like efficient businesses are more likely to develop romance and last longer than those that start out being purely romantic, never become practical, and wind up with the couple being disturbed, hysterical, angry, and wondering what the devil happened to their wonderful dreams.

Healthy and unhealthy reasons for marrying

If you accept my thesis that people marry in order to have a reasonable degree of satisfaction for their deep desires and needs, then the next important question we want to ask ourselves is just what are those deep desires and needs for which we marry?

In my experience there are about four healthy and broad reasons why we marry and about nine unhealthy reasons. I shall go over these points briefly, but anyone wanting to study this material more fully can consult my book, *Making Marriage Work*.

The healthy and mature reasons for marriage are:

Companionship

A mate should be your best friend. He or she is someone with whom you can talk over practically anything. He or she is some-one with whom you can gladly be alone for hours on end. He or she is someone with whom you simply feel as comfortable as an old shoe. Why would anyone want to give up such a person and let him or her enter and exit your life without trying to hold on permanently? When you have a good friend, you do whatever you can to cultivate the friendship and to be in the company of that friend for as many hours as you desire.

A safe and convenient sex life

This reason for marrying certainly should not be frowned upon; it is one of the unique contributions that a loving relationship has that other relationships often do not have. Sexual gratification is an integral part of all of our lives, even into the eighties and nineties. Most people marry with the full expectation that the relationship will bring forth pleasant and satisfying sex. Great stress is almost certain to result in the absence of sexual fulfilment.

If you have been true to your oath and have been faithful — both of you — the whole question of venereal diseases need never arise. In this day and age of genital herpes, a disease for which there is no known cure, who wants a sex life with a series of partners that is likely to give you such an infection?

A safe and sane sex life is also more likely with a couple who are married and who work out their sexual problems than it is with individuals who switch partners every few days, or months. It takes time to work out our sexual styles. But once our preferences have been communicated and our mates are used to them, we have created a situation in which we are comfortable with our partner's lovemaking.

Raising a family

Different societies and even modern-day governments have attempted to alter the traditional method of rearing a family. The Chinese have in some instances developed communal arrangements for the rearing of the young while the Israelites have their kibbutzim. From my reading on this subject I believe that these are not great improvements over conventional methods of rearing our children. In some instances a child might become more independent and not suffer the problems of living with a disturbed parent if the child is separated earlier and for greater periods of time in a state school or in a kibbutz. However, given a normal set of parents, there still seems to be no other method that truly equals the care, devotion, and end results we humans get when we raise our children ourselves.

Leaving aside the argument of positive effects on the children, raising a family also provides great pleasure and growth-promoting experiences for the parents. To become a parent is to relive your own life again. To sacrifice for children teaches you patience, endurance, and understanding. It may be wonderful for children to be raised by parents, but it is equally healthy for parents to have children they enjoy raising to maturity. The whole process is a growing, maturing, and fulfilling experience.

A unique lifestyle

The life a woman will lead depends in large measure on the man

she marries and the occupation he has. This is not to say that his
life is not influenced by the woman he marries. Obviously each
will have an enormously important effect upon the other. A
woman who marries a college professor will have a very different
life than she would if she married a physician or a bricklayer.

The lifestyle a person will lead depends largely on the earnings
of the couple, their educational backgrounds, and their social
skills. One of my clients whom I shall call Rose, married a
charming salesman who does a lot of travelling. Since neither
wanted children, they are able to travel together, spend time at
faraway resorts, invariably eat at the finest restaurants, and dress
in the latest fashions. She loves this kind of life, and so does he.
She wouldn't think of marrying anyone but a business man who
wears a white shirt and a tie and who can provide her with other
successful men and women as social companions. She has a very
nice home on the edge of the city, and gets a new car every year or
two. All-in-all she couldn't be happier.

Unhealthy reasons for marrying

There must be dozens and dozens of bad reasons for marrying
someone but it would serve no purpose to go over each one in
great detail. Here are some of the most common ones.

Fear of independence

Anyone who marries because he or she is afraid of becoming an
independent person marries for the wrong reason. When some
young people are about to grow up, to test themselves against the
world, to be on their own completely for the first time, they turn
tail on this experience and begin to doubt their own ability to
support themselves or live by themselves. Then they immediately permit themselves to fall into love. Notice that I use the
word 'permit'. After all, when we fall in love, it is because we
have allowed ourselves to have that emotion. This is not something that is forced upon us; it is something we permit, allow, and
talk ourselves into when it is convenient for us to have such an
emotion. One of the most convenient times, or so we think, is
when we are about to be cut loose from all of the normal supports
we have had while growing up.

Is it any wonder, therefore, that high school students often
marry shortly before or after graduation? It is because of their
excessive dependency, the fear of being alone, and their need to

lean on someone stronger than they that this decision is made. People who never have had some years of independence come to regret that they married too early.

To be a therapist for your mate

As you shall see in the coming chapters, one of the psychological faults which causes a great deal of misery in marriages is other-pity. It demonstrates itself in the need some men or women have to marry another person almost for the sole purpose of being able to cure that person of some difficulty. A woman may marry a man because he drinks or gambles; she believes that she loves him so much that she is going to cure him of this behaviour. Or a man may feel so sorry for a woman because she is down and out, can't handle her children, or is perpetually depressed that he sees himself as the knight in shining armour who is going to take her away 'from all that'.

Both of these people are making the same serious mistakes: they are marrying in order to be a therapist for the mate. Let me advise you never to do this. It usually doesn't work. Being the superior one in the relationship and suggesting that your partner is seriously troubled only makes that person more insecure and resentful over your sense of superiority. This leads to a backlash in the form of oppositional behaviour, making matters worse.

To spite your parents

There are few times in your life when it's harder to make a sensible decision than when you're a teenager. You are beginning to enter adulthood and want to think for yourself. Yet you don't have enough experience from life to make all the important decisions. This places teenagers in a bad spot because they will have to stick their necks out and make a lot of silly, unnecessary mistakes before they learn from the school of hard knocks. Unfortunately one of the more common occasions when children decide they are going to start thinking for themselves (rather than let themselves be advised by their parents) is when they consider getting married. Of all the times for them to reject parental advice, this is perhaps the worst. Parents are wrong about a great many things, and I'm the first to admit it. But when most parents advise kids not to get married too young, ninety-nine times out of a hundred they're right. However, because adolescents have to demonstrate to themselves and to the world that they are now capable of thinking without parental guidance, they often spitefully go ahead and marry just to prove they can do it. Little do prospective brides or grooms realize, when walking down the aisle, that they are trying to spite their parents. That is always a bad beginning for a marriage.

Fear of spinsterhood or bachelorhood

People frequently act recklessly while under the influence of fear. Those who anticipate they will have few opportunities for marriage may be so afraid of remaining spinsters or bachelors forever that they will say 'yes' to the very first offer without giving due consideration to the merits of the proposal. When desperate for marriage, people clutch for straws and marry almost anyone who will rescue them from what they consider to be the stigma of the unmarried state. As one of my clients once told me, 'I would have married anyone who asked me. I thought I was so unworthy that I would have considered myself lucky to get any invitation, much less the one I hoped for.' Needless to say, she had an unhappy marriage and eventually was divorced. She had married someone whom she would never (in her saner moments) have considered as a mate.

Social pressure is another reason why young folk are often self-conscious about not marrying. It is regarded as a failure on their part not to be attractive enough, or interesting enough, to gain a mate. When everyone around them is going down the aisle to the wedding march and they are still living the single life, the thought occurs to most of them that people are probably wondering what's wrong with them. The realization that it is perfectly mature for someone not to marry early in life, or never to marry at all, simply escapes them.

Because you were in love

I shall never forget counselling with a young fellow who was considering his third marriage and wasn't twenty-eight years old yet. I couldn't quite understand how he could get in and out of relationships so easily. From our further conversations I concluded that he had an irrational notion that convinced him that if he fell in love with somebody, he had to marry that person.

Falling in love is not the overpowering emotion that romantic literature and folk songs have led us to believe. It is a strong emotion to be sure, but it is one we talk ourselves into and one we can also talk ourselves out of. Love may be blind, but it is not the most powerful emotion that we experience. We *can* control it and we can fall out of love whenever we have a mind to.

To escape an unhappy home

One of the saddest reasons for marrying is, not because you are drawn towards a person, but because you are repulsed by another. A young boy or girl who cannot stand life at home will sometimes be attracted to the idea of marriage with such force that practically anyone can satisfy that need. Girls in particular are prone to use marriage as an escape from an unhappy home. Sometimes boys do it too. More often the young men become adventurous and hit the road, join the army, or hitchhike around the country.

I can fully appreciate the need for young people to get away from screaming parents, drunk or abusing fathers, nagging and demanding mothers. However, at times the fire the kids jump into is worse than the frying pan from which they leaped. Getting married at an early age and out of a sense of desperation is hardly the way to begin a peaceful and secure future. My advice is: if you are in such an intolerable situation that you feel you must leave, then leave. Try to have a job first, or live with a relative, or work for room and board. But don't get married just to escape from a home. All of the fears, the angers, the guilt and the inferiority which you have as a result of living in your intolerable home will go along with you right into the marriage bed. If you think you are going to start off a brand new relationship with a clean slate, you are absolutely mistaken.

The compatibility test

The principal question that you had better keep on asking yourself when you are falling in love with someone and deciding whether or not to marry is, 'Are we compatible?' Compatibility means that the two of you are on the same wavelength. The more compatibility the two of you have the better you will be able to get along. Keeping your finger on the pulse of your degree of compatibility is as important for your marriage as is stepping on a scale to check your weight in order to keep it within a desired range.

But what guidelines can we use to judge whether we are compatible or not? If you are compatible with your lover, you will answer these three questions in the affirmative.

Question 1. Does my partner *understand* my deepest desires and needs? To answer this question, I want you to write out what you feel are those major frustrations caused by your partner's behaviour which, if he changed, would make you feel considerably more loving towards him or her. Never mind how unrealistic your request might be at this point. Simply jot down what you feel your lover would have to do to make you less frustrated. The rationale behind this move is, of course, to repair any bad feelings between you. If your partner knows what your deep desires and needs are, and can satisfy them, then obviously you are more inclined to love your mate than if you are frustrated by your mate.

Question 2. Is my partner *capable* of satisfying my deepest desires and needs?

Some people who are incompatible are simply totally unable to please their partners in any significant way because they just don't have what it takes. If a woman has great artistic interests, loves to go to art galleries, attends the opera, and fills her house with oil paintings, she is probably not going to feel happily married to a man who throws darts in the local pub on Friday nights, and who enjoys watching football all Sunday afternoon. These two are simply not going to get along, not because he is a nasty fellow or because they hate each other, but because her interests are so vastly different from his. He may be incapable of satisfying her deep desires and needs to a degree that could bring her happiness.

Question 3. Is my partner *willing* to satisfy my deepest desires and needs?

Just because your lover may *know* what it takes to make you happy and be *capable* of fulfilling those desires and needs, does not necessarily mean that he or she will in fact *want* to make that effort. One man mentioned to me recently that he was fully aware of what his wife expected of him, and he knew that he was also perfectly capable of being the kind of husband she wanted him to be. But it no longer pleased him to be that way and therefore he had to say no to the third question.

As I mentioned previously, your partner is compatible with you if he or she can answer these three questions with a yes. A single no answer means that there is a degree of incompatibility which is going to give you trouble. I would suggest that you do not get married until those no answers change to affirmative ones. If you are married I would certainly urge you to clarify your frustrations and remove them as much as possible.

The goal of any caring relationship

When we come right down to it, the long and the short of rewarding human relationship depends on each party getting a reasonable amount of satisfaction from the other. People are not totally self-sacrificing; they expect some benefit in return. The question is, 'How much do you have a right to expect?' You have a right to be just reasonably content in any voluntary relation-ship. This is a point of emotional equilibrium which enables you to say that you are feeling fairly good about what's going on between you and your partner, that things aren't half bad, that you're glad you're married or in love, and that although you would still like a great many more things going your way, you can tolerate the situation without resentment if it doesn't get better than it is. The point at which you can say this to yourself is the point of *Just Reasonable Contentment* (JRC). The goal of a relationship is to see to it that you remain at least just reasonably content at all times and that you have hope for a greater degree of contentment. When the parties involved can all say that they are reasonably content there is obviously little reason to complain, and each party is bound to be pleased with the other party.

There are three serious consequences from allowing yourself to live in a state of frustration which is below your JRC.

The first obvious consequence is that you will generally be a disturbed, unhappy, and frustrated human being. If you are chronically dissatisfied, you are usually going to get depressed, angry, think of infidelity, bite your nails, sleep poorly, drink, or take your frustrations out on your children. You may use therapy to talk yourself into a reasonable state of calmness; but again, if your frustrations continue, you are simply not going to enjoy life a great deal even though you may not turn into a full-blown neurotic.

The second result of chronically living below your JRC is that you will most definitely begin to fall out of love with your partner. After all, what is there to be in love about if your partner, employer, or friend, is continually frustrating you? You have to be a seriously troubled person (and a desperate one besides) in order to continue to love someone who is mistreating you.

This loss of love usually happens rather slowly as the disappointments from one injustice and injury after another begin to pile up over the months and years. If there are not enough times when you are above your JRC you eventually are going to fall out of love with your partner. It doesn't matter how much you were in love to begin with, it doesn't matter what your religious faith is, it doesn't matter what your resolve is. Your feelings of love change eventually if you are not getting from your lover a reasonable amount of satisfaction.

Those of you who feel guilty over falling out of love are misinformed as to what is going on. It is not an evil thing to fall out of love. You don't have to feel guilty over rejecting others for their negligence. You are simply acting in a sensible, rational, and healthy way.

The third consequence of living below the JRC level on a chronic basis is that you will eventually not care about the relationship itself. When this happens in a job you eventually tell the boss to take his job and keep it. With a marriage you finally come to the conclusion that the whole thing isn't worth it anymore. You have lost all your feelings, and you say, 'I don't have to live like this anymore.'

Here, too, a great many people tend to feel guilty because they decide to end a marriage. But again, for exactly the same reasons they don't have to feel guilty for falling out of love, they also don't have to feel guilty when their marriages break up. When a marriage goes sour, and you won't change, it is your *duty* to do something about it. Remember that you are in a marriage, not for the other person's sake, but for your own. You didn't get a job to make your boss happy, you got a job to improve your own life. You marry, you become employed, you have a friendship, because it serves *your* purposes to have them. And when they don't do you any good you wisely want to withdraw from them. If a marriage is simply a waste of time to you, is creating hardships and no longer gives any pleasure, then thoughts of breaking up the marriage are bound to occur to you, and *rightfully so*. You are not doing anyone a favour when you sacrifice yourself for someone else's happiness while at the same time you are becoming a miserable human being. As a matter of fact, you are doing them a serious disservice because you wind up spoiling them, frustrating yourself, and getting fed up with them. Then one fine day you pack your bags and leave. If you really care so much about a relationship, frustrate it sometimes and train the people around you not to get you to despise them.

Accept the fact that a relationship exists happily because both people are reasonably pleased. When they are not, it is the duty, the moral obligation, of the person who is the most frustrated to do something to relieve the unhappy characteristics of the condition. That is the goal of a relationship: to make yourself reasonably content so that you do not want to end the relationship. Or to say it in a more practical way, to push the other party to give into you repeatedly for favour after favour until you can say to yourself that you are reasonably content. At that point you have serviced yourself and anyone else in the relationship, and you have done so in a moral and correct way.

3

The best way to achieve love

The best attitude to take when first encountering other people is to assume that they are fairly decent, that they mean you no harm, and that if you treat them well you will be treated fairly in return. That is the essence of Rule 1: when someone treats you nicely, reward that behaviour as soon as possible by treating that person nicely also.

This is known as positive reinforcement, one of the principles of animal and human learning theory as investigated in psychological laboratories throughout the world. When you reward a behaviour, that behaviour becomes strengthened. In psychological language we say the behaviour is reinforced. Stop and think for a moment what a powerful thing this is if you can use it correctly. If you know what is important to your partner, you can obviously make him or her enormously happy if you reinforce the behaviours that please that person.

Suppose you want your husband to lose weight so he will appeal to you more sexually? Keep Rule 1 in mind when dealing with him day in and day out. If he starts jogging, for example, and you do not make any comments about the jogging, he may lose heart and quit. Or suppose he deliberately pushes aside a serving of dessert and you do not praise him for his will power. Again you missed an opportunity to reinforce his dieting behaviour. It takes no genius to understand that if you want the man to continue to lose weight, you had better recognize his efforts by mentioning them at the very least.

Although this sounds like simplicity itself, it is actually a complicated subject. There are certain problems not immediately apparent in trying to be a reinforcing individual. Consider some of the following:

What is a reward?

We each define for ourselves what a reward is. You must not make the assumption that just because something pleases you enormously it will also please someone else. There are primary reinforcers such as food, water, sleep, warmth, and so forth which are necessary for physical survival. They are rewards for anyone most of the time. But whether a suit of clothing, a compliment, or a raise will serve as a reward depends upon the person who is receiving the reward, the age of the person, the personality of that person, and the particular events in that individual's life at the time the reward is being made. A fur coat to a woman who already has six is not very impressive. Taking a husband out to a restaurant on his birthday may be the last thing he wants if he is a travelling salesman and eats out ninety-five per cent of the time anyway. A reward for him would be a home-cooked meal.

The time of the reward

A reward and its effects depend not only upon the *kind* of reward it is but also *when* it was given. It is important that you be in a receptive mood for a reward in order for it to have its major effect. Making a meal for you when you are not hungry is simply bad timing. Giving you a rifle when you are thirty-five years old because you always wanted one when you were fifteen doesn't make sense either. Showing your appreciation by saying 'I love you' to your partner may also be badly timed if you are doing so after you have been asked for a particular favour a thousand times.

The frequency of the reinforcement

The effects a reward will have on us obviously depend upon how *often* the reward is made. If you want to influence your lover it is not only important that you give an appropriate reward, that you do it at an appropriate time, but also that you do it at a frequency which has the greatest impact. There are two ways that you can reward people: continuously, or intermittently. In the first case you are rewarding desirable behaviour every time it occurs. Naturally that behaviour will become strengthened rather rapidly. If you flatter and praise your partner for each kind act, each new article of clothing that looks attractive, and each time the partner looks particularly beautiful, a great deal of feeling is bound to be generated towards you because you are being so complimentary. However, when you are in the habit of making repeated rewards and then for some reason stop making them, the individual may immediately stop responding.

However, if you use *intermittent* reinforcement, you will

compliment only once in a while. Then, when your lover does not get a compliment every day he may still exercise repeatedly even though he is not being constantly rewarded. He anticipates that the behaviour *will* be reinforced in the near future.

Isn't it odd that when we reinforce behaviour on a less then constant basis it is harder to break that habit than it would be if we reinforce the habit 100 per cent of the time?

In summary, let us always be aware that to be loved one has to have a good idea of (a) what a reward is for the individual at this time of life, (b) that the reward interests that individual at this time of life, and (c) that we reinforce on a once-in-a-while basis (intermittently), not every time.

The most valued psychological rewards

If you want to be a loving person and get people to love you in turn, it is critical that you think of rewarding behaviour in practically all of your dealings with others. Sometimes it is essential that you know what the specific rewards are that appeal most to your lover. In general, however, you cannot go terribly wrong if you know what those behaviours are which simply appeal to most people under most circumstances.

Praise

I cannot emphasize how important praise is in influencing someone's feelings towards you. Most people who are praised for their actions repeatedly wind up with a sense of self-worth, feelings of self-confidence, and self-respect. They are not as affected by mistakes or rejection because they have been thoroughly programmed to believe that they are decent and worthwhile people. If you want someone to love you, I urge you to *accentuate the positive* and often to *ignore the negative*. It is almost impossible not to be influenced by someone who is treating you in this lovely and tender fashion.

We simply do not praise each other enough. We rationalize that we are 'being phonies', or 'there aren't that many good behaviours in people to justify constant praise'. Sometimes we are afraid we are going to spoil others rotten by pumping them up with too much recognition.

Before I make some comments about these three reasons why people resist giving praise, let me first explain what I mean by praise. I am referring strictly to complimenting a person on his or her *behaviour*, never *complimenting the individual personally*. It is essential that we separate *people* from their *behaviour* and then say something about their actions rather than about themselves. This is the very best way to give praise since it does not evaluate the person either positively or negatively. If this is done from the earliest years of a child's life, that child learns never to hate himself or herself because of bad actions and correspondingly never feels superior, conceited, or vain because of good actions.

When you understand this distinction between praising a person and praising a person's behaviour you can see why it is much easier to praise a person's actions if you bear in mind that your praise is not meant to let the person think he or she is better than others, only that a particular behaviour was better. In other words, if you like your partner's dancing, then why not say so? In fact, my advice to people who want to be loved and to demonstrate their love is to give in huge quantities. Say nice things to people. We hear those kinds of comments all too infrequently. People are only too willing to criticize each other rather than compliment each other. I maintain that you can compliment just as frequently as you can criticize. When something is done well, why not say something about it? Is your partner punctual? Compliment the punctuality (but not the person). Say 'Thank you', frequently. Get into the habit of noticing all those nice things people are doing for you but which you are taking for granted.

Those of you who insist you would feel like a phoney making numerous compliments are indeed making a bad excuse. Feel like a phoney if you must, but don't use that as an excuse for discontinuing the compliments. The feeling of phoniness arises essentially from this being new behaviour to you. You also feel like a phoney when you go out on the dance floor for the first time, or when you have to give a short speech to your civic club. Phoniness in these cases is nothing more than saying that you are unfamiliar with the task at hand. The more you practise the task, the better your skills become and the less 'phoney' you will feel.

What about spoiling people with compliments? If that actually happened I would be the first one to say not to do so. If you confine your remarks simply to a person's accomplishments, personality, material goods, talents, or intelligence, you will be separating the person from his attributes. That never leads to spoiling because no one is making comments about the total person.

Charm and tenderness

How can you dislike someone who is charming, considerate, tender and genteel? People who are refined, well-bred, polite, and not defensive, have to be the most sought after people in the world. What a pleasure it is to be in the company of someone who knows not only what to say and how to say it but also how to listen. Of all the social graces, these are undoubtedly the most highly prized.

If you want to love and be loved, learn to be charming, considerate, and tender. It is like sunshine on ice. Whose resistance and anger can withstand the warmth, the kindness, and the gentleness of an understanding and tender relationship? We have all known such people. They are sought after in greater numbers than the rest of us are. They have such an uncanny knack of making themselves liked that we thoroughly enjoy their company. We readily invite them to our homes, and we always think of them with a smile.

To love and be loved, learn these critical social techniques. But how can this be done? I have thought on this problem for quite some time and have concluded that the primary stumbling block against being a genteel individual is defensiveness. It is not so difficult to be a considerate and co-operative human being if you are not defensive. Defensiveness means that you are out to prove that you are always right, that the other person is wrong, and therefore must be shown up as being mistaken. I think people who are only too eager to point out your failings are a pain in the neck. They do not hesitate to find the weak spots in a person's character. To get a compliment out of them is like trying to separate a miser from his gold.

The undefensive person is more interested in keeping a relationship smooth than in being right. If a husband has made a statement with which his wife cannot agree, she does not hesitate to correct him. But if he will not accept that correction, she maintains that she still thinks she is right but could be mistaken and lets the matter rest there. What a nice thing to do! She has asserted herself, she has spoken her piece, and she is willing to let well enough alone because the whole issue is not worth fighting over.

Such people are liked precisely because they don't put people down when they disagree with them. They treat others gently and give them the benefit of the doubt. They are not wishy-washy or continually giving into others. Quite the contrary; they state their beliefs. But once they noticed that being found wrong would be highly threatening to the other person, they are willing to back off unless, of course, the issue is a critical one. The undefensive person is certainly not a coward.

A note for the men. I sometimes ask women what they find so appealing and attractive about a particular man whom many of them seem to like. Practically always the women who are particularly fond of a specific man say that he is charming, tender, and considerate. It makes little difference what he looks like, or how much money he has, or how well he dresses. I am convinced that most women like a man who is undefensive, knows what he believes and is willing to defend his viewpoint, but who readily gives in if it looks like bad feelings will be generated over an insignificant issue. These are the fellows who get all the respect and attention from the ladies, and it is a lesson I strongly urge all men to think about.

Deep desires and needs

In providing people with the rewards it takes to make them love you, nothing could be more important and pertinent than fully understanding their deepest desires and needs. These are the foundation stones of the love relationship you are trying to establish. It is my contention that if you are a complimenting, charming, and tender person, you will undoubtedly get your partner to feel very positive about you. However, to make your lover want to marry you, to live with you for the rest of his or her life, it is necessary that you not only be gracious and considerate, but that you have intimate knowledge of that individual's deepest desires and needs. Then, if you can satisfy those deep desires and needs to a *reasonable degree*, you will cause that person to be very fond of you. I specifically used the expression *deep* desires because the mere satisfaction of shallow desires does not lead to marriage. To fall deeply in love we must deal with deepest desires, not just surface desires.

Therefore, in order to be as rewarding as possible to your partner, discuss his or her deep desires and needs at some length. What is it that he wants from you? What it is that she wants? Talk these expectations over or write them down so you will not forget them. It is not until we write down these desires and needs and discuss them that we can get an idea of what the conditions are that will make this relationship a successful one.

Areas of conflict

Even if two individuals do understand their deepest needs and
desires, frustrations and conflicts are bound to arise. Bear in
mind, however, that, although you may have several or even
many frustrations you would like to see your partner remove, it is
still possible for you to be happy together if only one or several
major items are improved significantly. We cannot expect to get
everything we want, even though we deserve it. Where an issue is
not terribly important you may be able to give in to your partner
and ignore that matter. However, if an extremely important
desire is frustrated and you would feel cheated if you gave in
completely, I suggest that you learn to compromise. If you do
give in for that one, make sure you get your way almost totally on
another issue.

Marriage is a loving business, and, in my view, to make it work
we often have to sit around the table and negotiate our various
expectations with the same bargaining principles that labour and
management use. Keeping all of this in mind, let us look more
closely at several conflict areas:

1 *Financial responsibility*. When my clients complain about the
way their partners handle money, they generally refer to spending too lavishly, not balancing bank accounts properly, making
one-sided decisions on expensive items, not consulting with the
mate, or being very tightfisted. Women often complain about
their husbands wanting to control the purse strings and making
them come to him with hands out for grocery money, clothes, or
check-ups for the kids.

Men, on the other hand, sometimes complain that women
have a cavalier attitude about money as though it grows on trees.
When a woman is unhappy with the amount of money her
husband brings home, she may suggest in a rather naïve way that
he has to bring home more. Men complain that the ladies,
because they have sometimes not been out in the working world,
do not appreciate economic realities. They cannot bring home
more just because their wives wish it. The salary cheque is an
item often beyond a man's control and can only be improved with
gradual increases over a long period of time.

2 *Children*. Differences over rearing and disciplining children
can be one of the most stressful and powerful forces that create

difficulty with your mate. And this is readily understandable. Discipline, moral values, religion, self-discipline — these are all among the important characteristics parents want to develop in their children and over which they have some serious differences. A well organized man who tends to be consistent and who is not afraid to be firm with his children even though they may temporarily dislike him, may quickly lose respect for a wishy-washy mother. By the same token, a mother who has gentle and loving feelings for her children will be absolutely repelled by a husband who shakes his kids, yells at them, and screams at them because they won't clean up a small amount of food on their plates. She will wind up hating him thoroughly because of his rigidity.

Never underestimate the amount of distaste and disgust you can have for your partner if you don't respect that person as a mother or father of your children. That is why I urge you always to talk over your child-rearing practices and try to arrive at some agreement that you can live with.

3 *Sex*. The nature of the sexual relationship between a couple in love is absolutely critical to the survival of that relationship. Generally the feature which distinguishes a marriage relationship apart from a friendly relationship is the addition of the sexual element. Lovers are friends who sleep together.

Among the sexual desires and needs that men report most often in psychotherapy are: (1) the wish to have more sex, (2) for the female to take the initiative more often, and (3) for her not to require constant reassurances of his love through small acts of affection or repeated verbal declarations that he loves her.

Women also have a number of sexual preferences which, if they could be fulfilled by their lovers, would make them a great deal happier with their men. Generally, women do not like crudeness or bluntness. They like their sex clothed in softness. They want most sexual words to be words of love, not of sex. The raw expressions men often use are generally not appreciated. Women may sometimes use those profanities when they are angry, but when they are trying to be romantic and loving, they want to use the language of the poets, not the language of the street.

Women also like to take their time with their lovemaking. The wham-bam-thank-you-ma'am syndrome almost universally turns them off. This is because women respond more slowly and simply cannot get aroused with the same rapidity that is common among men.

Another major complaint women have is that they are expected to make love to their partners after an angry scene. It totally bewilders them that men want to take them to bed after they are called sluts and whores and other assorted vulgarities. Women make love with their hearts far more than with their bodies and if the feeling is not right, the sex is not right. I am absolutely convinced that if a man wants to be a great lover, he had better learn how to carry on his sex life with a great deal of affection. Women want the whole thing done correctly, not in some crude, disgusting fashion which treats their bodies as a piece of meat that is there to serve the lustful desires of an animal. I know few things that turn women off more than the refusal to understand this point. Women seem not to be interested so much in quantity of sex as in quality of sex.

4 *Church and religion.* Oddly enough people don't have as much conflict with each other over churchly or religious issues as one might anticipate. It seems as though there is a selective factor operating rather nicely before they get married which often prevents these conflicts. People who believe in God usually marry persons who have the same belief. Agnostics will be attracted to agnostics and atheists to atheists.

The most frequent complaint married couples give me concerning church and religious matters is the desire on the part of one of the partners to go to church more frequently as a family. Sometimes it is the mother who sees to it that the children have religious education, and sometimes it is the father. But neither one of them wants to take sole responsibility. However, even if there is a strong desire for family church activity and that desire is not met, this is seldom a major cause of stress between the two.

What causes more trouble are serious ethical and religious differences. When mother and father, for example, do not agree over such things as the existence of a god or the need to be accountable to a god, these serious issues can make living with one another rather strained. This is not always true, of course. I have known many couples who had vastly different religious backgrounds on the day they were married. True to expectation they had their ups and downs regarding these religious differences; but in many cases they adjusted to one another's views or decided to put religious issues aside and not let them interfere with the rest of their lives.

The ethical issues are every bit as serious as are the religious.

Divergent views on lying, stealing, and other moral issues are profoundly disruptive to a marriage. They are so powerful in fact, that compromise may not be possible. This difference sets it apart from other conflict areas that are usually negotiable.

5 *Relatives and in-laws.* Problems with relatives and in-laws may be frequent but when they exist they exist with intensity. The issue is usually the interference of relatives and in-laws in the marriage. Perhaps the husband is too closely tied to his parents and values their opinions over those of his wife. Or a wife can be so dominated by her mother and spend so much time over at her home that the husband feels he is not number one in her life.

6 *Work, job, occupation, or profession.* There are a number of ways in which the job of the husband or wife can interfere with marital happiness. Becoming aware of how these frustrations can interfere with your partner's deep desires and needs is crucial for developing feelings of love between the two of you.

Women complain most about the devotion men show towards their jobs. They often feel as though they are second to a man's profession or occupation. Men frequently bring work home, readily accept overtime assignments, or even busy themselves with chores around the house to such an extent that the women often feel ignored, rejected, and lonely.

A particular kind of work can also be a significant frustration in a marriage. Physicians are called on at all hours of the night. Their meals are interrupted, they are frequently not available for family holidays, and they often have rounds to make on Saturdays and Sundays. Any woman who marries a physician and is not ready to accept that kind of life-style is blind and foolish.

Being married to a truck driver or to a musician also has its built-in frustrations for the female. People in these occupations generally do a lot of travelling, or they work almost exclusively in the evenings — times when the wife would most like to have a man around the house. Some men work on the second or third shifts in large factories and this too can be a source of enormous frustration. It becomes even worse if the wife happens to be working a different shift.

In the same category of work and occupation is the frustration that women have over being just homemakers. Often they want to go back to school so that they can get a better job and do something more than sit around at home waiting for the kids to come home from school. This is sometimes a frightening experience for the woman because she will have been out of school for years and may not remember how to add fractions or take notes for a history course. Sometimes, however, the biggest obstacle she runs into is the reluctance of her chauvinistic husband to agree to let her further her education. Insecure men find ambitious women quite threatening. Not only are they sometimes afraid that their wives are really smarter than they are, but they also fear what would happen if their wives were to advance professionally, make good money, or socialize at the managerial level while the men remain at the labouring level.

Another difficulty arising out of work is that the man sometimes feels he has no obligation to help around the house because he puts in his eight hours in the factory. He is free, in his mind, to go bowling, hunting, golfing, or drinking because he has done his share. Women, of course, deeply resent this because in no way do they believe that putting in eight hours on a job frees them from any other family obligations. This is a macho idea that is going to have a hard time dying. If a man wants the love of his wife, however, he had better be aware of her bitterness over his thinking that his eight hours of work is somehow more important than her eight hours. And her objection will be that for her it isn't just eight hours; it's more like twelve or fourteen.

Socializing

In talking to troubled couples and in going through this list of deep desires and needs I am surprised at how often both parties want to have more of a social life. This seems to be a difficult thing for many of them to achieve. Sometimes one of the couple has good social skills and seems to arrange all the social functions. The other is happy to follow along but often cannot be the initiator who meets the people or makes the suggestions for a social get-together. I find that those marriages that have a fair amount of social life in them are among the happier ones. It gets to be pretty boring simply going to a movie with the kids or with your partner week after week. Many couples who otherwise would be terribly bored at home can cure that simply by knowing that on Friday night, Saturday night, or Sunday afternoon, something is cooking and they will be attending a party, a small dinner, or just a drive with another adult couple. The couple that socializes together, stays together.

Irritating and annoying habits

Ask yourself if your mate has irritating and annoying habits that seem trivial on the surface but can be so annoying to you at times that you could start a fight over them. Among the examples that I have come across in my practice are: people squeezing saliva through their teeth and making hissing noises, others sniffing all the time rather than using a handkerchief. I have come across a great many women who object to their husbands telling obscene jokes in polite company or using profanity in inappropriate settings.

Annoying or irritating habits are usually not so serious as to cause a marriage to break up. If several bad habits exist, however, and if they are offensive enough, they too can be every bit as serious as some of the other objections we have already studied.

A few cautions

To give you a better idea of what some people consider serious frustrations in a marriage, let me go through my records for a moment and pick out some of the objections my clients have expressed to me:

1 Think of me as a capable individual, not someone you need to yell at all the time.
2 Tell me where you go when you leave the house.
3 Include me in the financial matters in the family.
4 Make the children more responsible by being more consistent with the penalties you set for them.
5 Tell me what your sexual desires are and what more I can do to please you.
6 Don't be so rejecting of my mother.
7 Let's go out more. You find the babysitters sometimes.
8 Be more affectionate without sex.
9 Don't take out your hidden resentments against our son.
10 Don't embarrass me with your outspokenness in social situations.
11 Do more together, such as go to church and enjoy it.
12 Give more of yourself when you come home from work.
13 Stop drumming your fingers all the time.
14 Enjoy my music or tolerate it.
15 If you don't want sex don't give it and then blame me later.

16   Stop biting your nails.
17   Take better care of our things.
18   Tolerate my work and appreciate the lifestyle it gives us.
19   Be more organized and punctual.
20   Stop turning my statements around.

There you have a considerable list of examples of how people have complained about their mate's behaviour. When I was able to get these objections removed or reduced, the feeling of love towards the other party practically always increased. This should come as no surprise since it follows Rule 1: if somebody does something nice to you, do something nice to them.

Special techniques you can use to earn more love

In addition to the highly rewarding behaviours pointed to previously, ones that are likely to bring out feelings of love, let us focus on some important techniques usually regarded as love-producing actions.

Determine the physical and emotional tolerance for intimacy in your lover

I once had a very charming couple to dinner at my home, and when the woman said goodbye she had her face so close to mine that I was immediately uncomfortable. There was nothing sexual in her act; that was simply the way she began or ended visits with practically anyone. She liked being up close. If two people happen to enjoy the same intensity of intimacy they have a great advantage over those who have to work this out by trial and error.

Some couples present this dilemma quite clearly. One man does not like to sit next to his wife, nor does he enjoy holding her hands in public, and does not like to show affection if he does sit next to her on the couch. Yet he loves her deeply, treats her very fairly and lovingly, and is in every other respect a mature and decent human being.

His wife, on the other hand, complains bitterly that she does not get enough affection and touching, petting, hugging, or kissing from him. She wants a great deal more intimacy than he tends to give. It would make her happy if he would pat her, rub her, hug her, or squeeze her every time he walked by her. She would think that she was getting a massage standing up and she would love it. Since she gets nothing of the sort, the woman is quite unhappy and does not know what to do. The answer of course is that if he cares for her he is going to have to make more of an effort to overcome his physical aloofness and make the physical contact. She wants touching, and nothing short of that will do. Or she can convince herself perhaps that it isn't so necessary after all to be as intimate as she likes and that he offers so much else in the marriage that there is no need to make a fuss over this one neglected area. One or other of these plans will have to work if the marriage is to succeed. To ignore this vital issue is to invite serious frustration, and unhappiness.

The words you use

What people say and how they say it is not the most important thing in the world. To me what people do is a great deal more important than what they say they will do. Nevertheless, when we think of the best ways to achieve love, we must recognize that words *are* significant. It happens that, in some of our dealings with each other, what we say and the way we say it is enormously important and has a great deal to do with whether we earn the love of others.

Some people find it very difficult to say: 'I love you.' Yet, there is something almost mystical and almost magical about that phrase. When people hear those 'three little words' said with sincerity they have a feeling of reassurance, warmth, and good will that is seldom achieved in any other way.

Nasty and vulgar words have as much impact in a negative direction as kind and gentle words have in a positive way. If you want to love and be loved, you had better avoid harsh obscenities, put-downs, the yelling. Think particularly about yelling. Yelling suggests to the listener that the degree of displeasure, irritation, and annoyance is reaching the point of danger. Why is it that all listeners to yelling are aware of this danger but the ones doing the yelling are not? Men in particular, but mothers also, often do not understand how their wives or their children take snarling as a very threatening sign. They do not seem to see how others can become so frightened that they lose their self-assurance and become anxious, worried, or even panicky.

Some women do not have the strength to demand their way with men and therefore use gentler and less violent means. Women often have verbal skills superior to those of men; and I can't blame them for resorting to nagging to get their way. What else can they do that is equally effective?

Used with reason and rationed with wisdom, nagging can act like the work of a good fairy godmother prodding us always on to proper action. But overdone, ah, that's another story. Some wives can tell you how they unwisely kept pressing their concerns with endless and unceasing nagging until the patience of their husbands was completely exhausted. Then they found themselves pushed against the wall, heels six inches off the floor, their husband's left hand around their necks, and right fists cocked back to their shoulders, ready to shut them up forever.

The dangers of overlove

It may appear strange in a chapter on the best ways to achieve love that I now recommend the keeping of one's kind behaviour in check. Strange as it may seem, there is ample evidence in the experience and practice of established therapists to indicate that being too good, is not good.

A middle-aged divorced woman did a very creditable job of raising her three children until her husband divorced her. The children were all of an age that they could choose with whom they wanted to live; and, much to her surprise, they all opted to live with their father. My client was actually a very devoted mother, very responsible, totally concerned with the welfare of her children, and could not understand how they could turn her down when a choice had to be made between her, the loving mother, and him, the normally disciplining father.

What hurt even more was the degree of detachment she received when she moved a few streets away and realized that her children would not call her up frequently, would not stop by to visit her, and in effect treated her as though she lived 200 miles away. She could never claim they were hostile towards her, or that they did not love her. It was simply that they showed no sense of appreciation for what she had done for them, and repeatedly treated her in a rather matter-of-fact way. That hurt the most.

When you love a child or an adult who is capable of returning your favours (but you do not require them to do so) it is my contention that those people will like you, but not love you. Those who perform services for which no return is expected (except perhaps money) are not people who are usually loved. These individuals become employees of ours; and although we may appreciate their loyalty, once they leave us we can accept their departure with little regret. We often feel no need to demonstrate further caring for them because they have been paid off.

To create a *mutual* experience of love between two people requires that the deep desires and needs of *both* people be satisfied. When only one party is rewarded, that party is a servant and other is the master. I concluded that my client, and anyone else who is continually giving without receiving, is a servant.

And just how could my female client have received reciprocal love from her children? I believe she overloved them when they neglected her. She failed to withhold her services until she was reimbursed, so to speak, with similar services from them. The withholding of affection, services, or favours, can start out gently, but must always have the potential of making the other person uncomfortable for being neglectful. This is where you get your power to influence the relationship on your behalf. It is when you begin to withhold your *total* acceptance and make getting along with you a *conditional* thing, that you demonstrate your capacity to create concern, frustration, or even fear in your lover. You are saying by these frustrating acts that you will not tolerate shabby behaviour, that you expect a reasonable amount of consideration from your lover, and that if this is not forthcoming, you are perfectly prepared to reject that person in major ways, or completely.

Once your partner or children understand that you have the power to make them uncomfortable and to regret their neglecting you, they are likely to become aware of what it is you want, and what it is that they had better do in order to get you away from your nasty attitude. In short, unless they begin to satisfy some of your deep desires and needs, you will make their lives uncomfortable because they cannot succeed in getting you to show your love for them.

Can you now see why a person who is totally giving and expects nothing in return for his or her services, is often not a truly loved person? Total acceptance breeds that kind of onesidedness. Conditional acceptance, on the other hand, practically forces the other party to consider you and to make your relationship a give and take process in which much more is involved than a few simple services or the exchange of money.

All of us have observed that those people who seem to be respected the most are those who put up with nonsense the least.

While on the contrary, those who are very yielding, submissive, and humble, are often trod upon and easily taken advantage of by people who pounce at the chance of getting as much out of a relationship as they can.

My recommendation to all you saints is that (with the exception of your relationships with infants, helpless animals, and elderly persons) you make your love conditional. Do not give it away for nothing. In order to love and be loved, learn to make your partner, parents, or children somewhat uncomfortable with you if they neglect you. Do this not only for your sake, but also for theirs. I say 'their sake' because I consider it unfortunate and wrong to raise children, to live with parents, or to engage in a romance without insisting that others show themselves to be reciprocating and sharing persons.

Mock protest

There is another complex dynamic between lovers which also hinges on too much love. This often affects well-meaning men who erroneously believe that giving their partners everything they want is the royal road to romantic success. The more you please someone in practically every way, the more certain you are to have a warm and secure loving relationship, so the thinking goes. It has been my experience that not only is it healthy to disagree with your partner and say 'No' every so often, but that women in particular *want* their male companions to reject some of their requests.

To understand your female companion and to get her to love and respect you more it is important that you appreciate the fact that one of the things she wants in a man is that he be strong, ready to make decisions, and a leader on whom she can rely in a tight spot. She looks for strength in her partner.

Women test men by making themselves the guinea pigs. They will give him a bad time and become uncooperative, difficult, and sometimes just plain flighty, to see what the old boy is going to do about it. If he shrugs his shoulders or slinks away she discovers what she was afraid of: that her so-called protector has weak knees. What she was hoping for all along was that he would stand up to her, show her that he is strong enough to live without her, and that if she rejects him because he cannot or will not please her in every way imaginable, she can very well pack her bags and leave. This is secretly what she wants him to do, because it will prove to her that this man is not a sissy, he has courage, and even she cannot shake him. That realization, that she is not necessary to his existence, and that she cannot wrap him around her finger is precisely what she is hoping to find out. Pity the man who wants his partner's love so badly that he gets shaky and gives her everything she wants. Little does he realize that he is losing her respect with every inch that he sinks to his knees.

When he does stand up for himself and refuses to be a marsh-mellow, the woman often screams her head off. She protests loudly that he is being unreasonable, that she deserves what she asks for, that he doesn't love her, and so forth. And the man, seeing all this storm and fury, may feel that his romance is in danger and decide to give in. This is a mistake. What he inter-prets as a totally rejecting attitude on the part of the woman is still part of her experiment. She has to see whether or not he can stand the heat. What does it take to get him to give in? Will the arguing and accusations weaken the man? If he stands up to her and does not give into emotions and protests, he reassures her that he is an adult, a mature, and strong human being who is not easily swayed by unreasonable and hysterical arguments.

Three exceptions

I have shown that in order to love and be loved, it is critical that you learn to satisfy your partner's deepest desires and needs but, even before this, that you understand *what* those deep desires and needs are. Most of the time this is not a difficult matter and might even be learned over a cup of coffee. But sometimes, unfortunately, what it takes to get a person to love you is totally unsuspected. Men need to learn that when they make advances to women, there are exceptions to expected responses.

We have generally been taught that women can be turned on by flattery, jewellery, flowers, candlelight and wine dinners, and all the lovely courtesies that go into seduction. Seduction is the immediate technique men think of when attempting to be suc-cessful lovers. This approach works quite well, *but* only when the woman is in a fairly receptive mood for being seduced.

What is not so generally understood is the power of non-sexual behaviour to accomplish the same end. This should not surprise you if you continually bear my definition of love in mind, namely, that we love those who make us happy. Therefore, if a woman would be made very happy to have the children taken to a movie so she can have an afternoon completely free to take a bubble bath and do her toe nails, then this becomes an act of seduction. A man who performs these services for her time and again will generally be highly regarded by her. She will think of him as considerate, tender, and very loving. And when a woman is loved she usually becomes amorous also.

This means that a man doing dishes for his wife, helping vacuum the living room, taking her car to the garage to have the oil changed, doing her grocery shopping, or simply talking to her, may lead to the bedroom more quickly than ugly arguments and complaints about not enough love and sex. The sexiest place in the house is not the bedroom, it is practically anywhere else. And the preparation for a sexual evening had better not begin as the two of you are walking towards the bedroom. It is much more successful if it starts in the morning at breakfast.

A second exception to expected behaviour that sometimes baffles men is that women do not necessarily enjoy sexual fondling the way men do. To a woman, if she is not in the mood, this is like mosquitoes bothering her when she is taking a sun bath. To have an adoring husband come up behind her when she is at the stove and for him to put his arms around her from the back and fondle her gently is often more of a pain in the neck than it is a pleasure to her heart. Women sometimes simply do not want to be bothered with sexual advances. They feel as though they are being mauled when men are always after them.

The third exception that men discover is that no matter what they do with some women, the females' prior conditioning and sexual programming may have been so distorted that nothing the man does can get them to relax sexually. Women who have been raped, who have experienced incest, rejection by other lovers, or who have other emotional problems can be enormously difficult to love. It is not necessarily a situation you have created, and it is not a situation which you are necessarily perpetuating. It is a problem which simply exists because she had those problems before you met her. And getting her to give them up may be beyond your skills or the patience which is required.

Women who go through sexual traumas can develop problems of a masochistic type, some become promiscuous, and others develop sexual inhibitions. The most typical feminine reaction to cruel male behaviour is a loss of trust in men, shown as a fear of intimacy. Unless you have seen or experienced fear of intimacy it is difficult to appreciate how absolutely cautious women *and* men can be about allowing themselves to become vulnerable again.

Those of you who have partners who fear intimacy had better learn to be extremely patient people. Your sex partners are usually not rejecting you out of spite. They simply have been hurt, and their trust has been so shaken that it simply takes a great deal of time to get over their fear. If you behave in haste with such a partner, you are going to lose the goal you so strongly desire; but if you are patient, willing to make progress an inch at a time and then to accept relapses, and to do this week after week and month after month, you may find that in time your efforts are handsomely rewarded. Woe to you however, if you get angry, yell, threaten to leave, or call your frightened partner unflattering names. Those are precisely the techniques that led to the problem in the first place and those are exactly the techniques that can prolong the problem.

Summary

In this chapter I have introduced the enormous powers of reinforcement learning. Of the rules for achieving co-operation, respect, and love, this is the most beautiful, and often the most effective.

Rule 1 states that if someone does something nice to you, do something nice in return. I have tried to show the particular behaviours other people prize if you want them to love you, but I have also identified particular behaviours about which you sometimes can do very little even though you are trying to create reciprocal acts of love. Rule 1 does not always work, obviously, and it is important that you accept the fact. If reinforcement were always successful, there would be no need for rules two and three.

Remember also that, generally speaking, the more you reinforce behaviour the stronger it gets. When behaviour exists you can make the solid assumption that it exists because it is being reinforced by someone. You may not know who is reinforcing and rewarding certain behaviours because this is sometimes done in a very subtle manner. Nevertheless, if what you are doing does not create desired changes of behaviour, you had better look more deeply into your own actions or look very closely at the actions of others who unknowingly may be rewarding undesired behaviour.

The question may naturally be occurring to you, 'What do I do if someone treats me badly?' That will be the topic of our discussion in the next two chapters.

4

The other cheek

The second rule for achieving co-operation, respect, and love is this: If others treat you badly, treat them nicely for a *reasonable* period of time.

You may perhaps notice that the above statement reflects, in part, the message of Christianity. It suggests that when people treat us badly we must first be patient with them, love them despite their sins, turn the other cheek, go the extra mile, sit down and reason with them, and give them time to make changes. This is a beautiful message and implicitly always gives our frustrators the benefit of the doubt. In utilizing Rule 2 we assume that we have been wronged, trespassed against, and frustrated: not out of vindictiveness, not out of evil or hostility, but out of misunderstanding and ignorance. That is why we do not immediately want to attack, reject, or treat others disrespectfully because they have behaved in an unacceptable way. We make the assumption that an explanation can get them to understand us better. We hope that by being patient, the frustrator's behaviour will change through enlightenment. We rightfully expect that if we treat them nicely they will lose their defensiveness and appreciate our sacrifice and return our loving act with their own loving behaviour. Literature is full of examples of negative behaviour being turned into positive behaviour by the big-heartedness of the person who actually did the suffering.

To achieve this degree of patience and understanding, to be able to control our own natural neurotic and destructive emotions when we are wronged, is not an easy task. Loving your enemies or accepting the sinner even though you reject the sinning, are skills which can be learned through a great deal of hard work.

In the final analysis we are unforgiving and impatient human beings when we are disturbed emotionally. Those who are impulsive, panicky, jealous, or poorly self-disciplined, have the greatest need for serenity when under attack. The more stable you are, the more loving you can be when those around you are unstable. One of the quickest ways in the world to create more neurotic behaviour and more injustice is to get just as upset as your wrongdoer. There is very little likelihood of your being an

accepting and patient person who can let another person grow
(despite an unacceptable experience) if you yourself are hostile,
bitter, and hysterical. You will not get good results from treating
nicely those who treat you badly unless you learn to control your
emotions. In this chapter, therefore, I offer a short course in
psychopathology and to hit the highlights of what you should
know about the way emotional disturbances are created and how
you overcome them. For fuller expositions of this material I refer
you to some of my other books — which include volumes on
overcoming various problems as well as the book on assertion
entitled *How to Stand Up for Yourself*, the one on marriage,
Making Marriage Work, and the one on self-discipline, *How to
Do What You Want to Do*.

The four options

Before going into an actual description of how we create our
emotional problems and what we can do about them or how
these emotions interfere with our achieving respect and love, I
want you to appreciate why neurotic behaviour is so damaging.
There are four choices you have in dealing with very frustrating
situations. Neurotic behaviour is one of those choices, and it is
the one option I do not recommend. You have three other and
better options:

Option 1: Toleration without resentment

The first avenue of approach we often take in dealing with
people's difficult behaviour is that of toleration without resentment. We tend not to make too much of behaviour we do not
like, we accept it gracefully, we tend to minimize its seriousness,
and we convince ourselves, if possible, that it is not a big issue and
that we might just as well keep our mouths shut.

We do this many times in our lives, and I think it is wise that we
do so. Many of the frustrations we encounter from day to day are
hardly worth starting World War III over; and, therefore, we
might as well ignore minor irritations and simply tell ourselves
'That's life.' Whenever you do this you immediately end the
frustration because you are convincing yourself there isn't any
frustration over which it is worth being upset. If not used to
excess, this is an extremely mature approach to personal difficulties, and it often shows you off as the more grown-up of the
individuals involved. You are someone who has the patience and

tolerance not to permit yourself to be unduly frustrated over minor issues.

Option 2: Protest

If tolerating things without resentment begins to become more difficult because the frustrations never seem to end, you may want to stop being endlessly patient. Now you do not turn the other cheek, but do the opposite. You protest, make the other person uncomfortable, become so difficult that he or she begins to see how serious the issue is and how behaviour is going to have to change because you are so annoyed. In using this strategy you go on *strike* or declare a *cold war* until you get what you want.

If this does not achieve its goals and you find yourself becoming very unhappy because of the great tension produced by this cold war, you still have the choice of going back to your first option. You can lump this situation gracefully and without resentment with those really not worthy of distress or you can go on to your next option.

Option 3: Separation or divorce

You don't have to stay with most situations if you don't want to. Fortunately we usually have a choice of staying or not staying with a job, keeping or not keeping a friend, or preserving or not continuing a marriage.

Separation and divorce now are recognized as proper and fortunate options all of us have at our disposal. When we can no longer tolerate inappropriate behaviour, and when it does no good to fight for our rights because of another person's resistance, then what other option does a sane person have? The only healthy thing to do then is to leave the unhealthy relationship if one can possibly do so.

Option 4: Toleration with resentment

Possibly the most frequent method used by all of us in dealing with negative behaviour is simply to get disturbed openly or to let our feelings stew inside and cause physical symptoms. When we tolerate situations or behaviours but deeply resent them, we are laying the ground work for psychosomatic complaints of all kinds. This is the way we get headaches, stomach aches, colon problems, sleep disturbances, and nervousness. This is how we become depressed, angry, lose interest in life, or develop excessive passivity. We may begin to drink too much and eat too much, or we may not eat enough. Perhaps we begin to have sexual fantasies or actually become unfaithful. And maybe we only bite our nails and cry a little. In any event, the more we tolerate frustrations but continue to resent them, the more we are going to become disturbed. This is not a good way to cope with inappropriate behaviour. It is in fact the only option of the four which I strongly recommend that you *never* use.

The first three options, though they may cause difficulty for a time, offer hope of eventual relief, by tolerating something without resentment we in fact end the pain almost instantly. By protesting and making our partners uncomfortable until they change, we may go through hell for a while; but most of the time this too brings an end to our suffering. And the same may be said for a separation or divorce. At first this option can be very disruptive and painful, but eventually we pick up the pieces of our lives and very often have better relationships than we had before. It is Option 4, however, that offers no relief to us. To become resentful and develop all kinds of bad symptoms simply makes our condition worse than it ever was before.

We need, therefore, to learn how not to develop these emotional problems. This is important for two reasons. In the first place, it is painful to be neurotic. Whenever you are upset you are usually hurting yourself more than anyone else. Secondly, it is hard to be a mature person, to follow Rule 2, and in return for rude and inconsiderate behaviour to offer loving and kind behaviour if you are very disturbed. We ought to have mature control over ourselves if we are to follow the noble guidance of Rule 2, which is to love our enemies and go the extra mile. Disturbed people cannot do that. But people who have fine emotional control do it often and do it more easily.

In the rest of this chapter let us consider further two of the options for dealing with frustrating situations: Option 1, Toleration without resentment, and Option 4, Toleration with resentment. We need to learn how to eliminate the latter and achieve the former. This is essentially what it means in practical terms to follow Rule 2, 'turn the other cheek', as a method to achieve love.

The next chapter will discuss the other two options for dealing with frustrating situations — Option 2: Protest; and Option 3: Separation or divorce. These are ways for following Rule 3 for achieving co-operation, respect, and love: if someone does something bad to you, and being reasonable has not worked, do something bad to him or her.

How we upset ourselves

If we are to tolerate frustrations without resentment, we must learn that emotional disturbances are caused by the way we talk to ourselves about our problems. It is our thoughts that cause us to be depressed, angry, fearful, or jealous. It is not the way people behave towards us that creates these feelings; it is what we make of them.

Simply put, there are twelve irrational ideas that cause practically all of the normal emotional disturbances. Depression is caused by one set of two or three such thoughts. Anger is created when we maintain several other irrational thoughts; and fear and worry, jealousy, procrastination, and passivity also derive from sets of irrational thoughts. If you are ever disturbed it is important that you try to detect how you are talking to yourself *about* your problems, then decide among the thoughts you have those which are reasonable and those which are not. Lastly, talk yourself out of believing the foolish and irrational ideas. This, in addition to leading you to practise new behaviour, will make you feel differently and cause you to be undisturbed.

The twelve irrational ideas

There are twelve irrational ideas with which we upset ourselves and keep us from tolerating frustration without resentment. If you commit to memory these ideas; you can, whenever you are upset, quickly put your finger on one or a group of the ones that could be causing your painful emotion.

1 Irrational Idea No. 1: It is absolutely necessary that we adults be loved and approved by the important people in our lives if we want to consider ourselves worthwhile.
2 Irrational Idea No. 2: If we are not outstanding, accomplished, and achieving, we are less worthy than those who are.
3 Irrational Idea No. 3: People who are bad, wicked, or villainous, must be severely blamed and punished for their wickedness.
4 Irrational Idea No. 4: It is awful and unbearable when things are not the way we would very much like them to be.
5 Irrational Idea No. 5: Human unhappiness is caused by external circumstances; thus we have little or no ability to control our sorrows and disturbances.

6 Irrational Idea No. 6: If something is or may be dangerous or
   fearsome we should be terribly concerned about it and keep
   dwelling on the possibility of its occurring.
7 Irrational Idea No. 7: It is easier to avoid certain life difficulties and self-responsibilities than it is to face them.
8 Irrational Idea No. 8: It is reasonable and healthy to be
   dependent upon others who are stronger than we are and on
   whom we can rely.
9 Irrational Idea No. 9: Our past history is an all-important
   determiner of our present behaviour; if something in the past
   once affected our lives it will continue to do so indefinitely.
10 Irrational Idea No. 10: We should become quite upset over
   other people's problems and disturbances.
11 Irrational Idea No. 11: There is invariably a right, precise,
   and perfect solution to human problems and that it is wiser to
   do nothing until the right answer has been found.
12 Irrational Idea No. 12: Beliefs held by respected authorities
   or society must be correct and should not be questioned.

There you have practically all of the major irrational ideas that
can lead to emotional problems. These statements, or some
variation of them, are the ones with which we knowingly feed
ourselves whenever we are confronted with a situation. And, the
particular irrational idea or ideas that we put together create
different emotions, just as the various ingredients a cook uses in
the kitchen determine the final outcome of a meal. If you want to
be a stable person, learn to question these ideas for their sound-
ness and their logic. I maintain they are all illogical, irrational,
foolish, and ultimately self-defeating. These irrational ideas contribute to depression, with its specific causes — self-blame, self-
pity, and other-pity; and they contribute also to anger and fear.

Depression

Psychological depression comes from three acts: self-blame,
self-pity, and other-pity.

Whenever you put yourself down, hate yourself, think that you
are worthless, and feel terribly guilty over some unacceptable
act, you tend not only to disapprove of what you have done but
also to disapprove of yourself as a total human being. That is
what I call self-blame. Self-blame is a double attack, first, on our
actions, then ourselves. We seem to find it extremely difficult to

separate our behaviours from ourselves and therefore frequently feel inferior, guilty, and depressed whenever we behave in a manner we disapprove.

To overcome guilt, inferiority, and self-blame, it is important to perform two separate mental tasks. The first is to separate your behaviour from yourself; the second is to forgive yourself for having done badly.

How can you separate your actions from you? In the same way that you often do it for others. You even do it for animals. If your puppy messes up the house you're inclined to disapprove, but you would hardly hate the dog. If a baby knocks over a valuable piece of pottery you can certainly regret the fact that the vase was broken, but you certainly don't have to conclude the child was terrible for breaking it.

Your second important task is to forgive yourself for what you have done even if you are not hating yourself for a hateful act. Your erroneous behaviour arises because you are *deficient, ignorant,* or *disturbed.* For example, you might not have the speed or co-ordination to be a boxer or a tennis player. Or you may never have been taught these skills. Or you may be so upset that you cannot possibly perform well.

If you are able to conquer self-blame you will find that it will be a great deal easier for you to tolerate other people's behaviour without resentment. You can ask yourself what your mate's problem is and why he or she behaved badly. Was your partner deficient, ignorant, or disturbed? How is it possible to be bitter and resentful toward anyone if you forgive yourself and others?

Another benefit derived from overcoming a sense of guilt is the ability to seek and hold on to self-respect. This is a vital quality that all of us seek in other people and that makes us love them, often intensely. People who do not have self-respect usually lose the respect of others. If you refuse to hate yourself for anything, and if you never think you are evil, worthless, or rotten, you are certainly not likely to experience the pains of guilt and inferiority. Instead, you will be holding your head high, your shoulders back, and thinking proudly of yourself even though you are not always proud of what you have done. Such people are to be admired and usually are. Most importantly, they can turn the other cheek without resentment.

Self-pity

The second major way in which we depress ourselves is self-pity. This is an extremely common method despite the fact that most of us are ashamed to admit it. Still, it occurs in us all. And for good reason. This world we inhabit is seldom the hospitable and wonderful paradise we dream of. It is sometimes cruel, often vicious and even more frequently totally unjust. The criminal can literally get away with murder while the desperate and hungry man is sent to prison for stealing just enough food to keep himself alive.

The moment you pity yourself more than just a little bit, try to appreciate the fact that you have just then enormously worsened your life. Self-pity is fruitless. It incapacitates you. It drains you of the energy to challenge the injustices of this world. And it gets people to leave you alone so that you can nurse your miseries by yourself.

One of the by-products of self-pity is that those with whom we live become impatient with us. No one likes a cry-baby, a whiner, or a complainer. It is far better to work diligently, even feverishly, to change these unkind events if we possibly can, or to accept them with resignation if we cannot. The person who shows the maturity not to collapse in a flood of tears, or to become hysterical, or to be seriously depressed as though that were going to accomplish a positive end, will earn love and respect. By conquering self-pity we are in an excellent position to face our frustrations and, in facing them, to practise Option 1: toleration without resentment.

Other-pity

The irrational idea that leads to the sad emotion of other-pity is this: 'One should be upset and disturbed over other people's problems and disturbances.'

Why should we? What conceivable good do we do for others when we allow ourselves to become upset because of their misfortunes? Does it help them? How? Does it give them courage to go on, or does it rob them of the sense of confidence and the courage to go on, or does it rob them of the sense of confidence and the courage to overcome adversity?

Caring and being concerned about someone else's plight is a healthy and ethical stance to take when others are in trouble. We can offer them our assistance, help them to get back on their feet, and be our brother's keeper as we are urged to do by our religious teachings. However, when we become *over-caring, over-concerned,* and feel *too much* for the suffering of others, we often don't do everything we can for them because we are joining them in their misery. Perhaps misery loves company, but it certainly doesn't do much to solve problems.

Anger

Anger is another of the common emotional problems that troubles practically everyone. Anger arises essentially because we say to ourselves the same thing that the self-pitier does: 'It is terrible and awful when I do not get everything I want.' But, in addition, another irrational thought is added: 'People are bad and wicked, and should be severely blamed and punished for frustrating me.' This combination leads to bitterness, resentment, hatred, aggression, and, of course, anger.

Anger is always caused by ourselves, not by someone else, just as psychological depression is caused by ourselves, never by others. The angry person unfortunately believes that because he is a decent and fair person he not only would *like* to have what he wants, would *prefer* it, *desire* it, and *wish* it, but also the things he wants are *needs, necessities*, and *demands*. When you convert your wishes to demands and you are not given what you demand, you will suffer the consequences of anger. If you had kept your wishes at the level of the wish and then been frustrated, you would simply have been disappointed or regretful. No one ever gets mad because he or she did not get what was wished for. Ask yourself how many wishes you have had in your lifetime and how many of them have never been satisfied. And how many times did you get angry over the fact that you did not discover a million dollars in your backyard? Or that you were not made a movie star last week? Or that you are not famous? These are all wishes; there are thousands of them, but we are never truly angry when they are not satisfied. When however, even for an instant, we insist that we *should* have our wishes fulfilled, and think that because we are right we must have our way, we then have made a *neurotic demand* out of a *healthy* wish and we suffer a neurotic emotion.

If you never wanted to get angry again in your whole life, it would be theoretically possible to achieve this goal by simply never making another demand out of any of your wishes.

There are two exceptions to the rule that anger is always neurotic. The first is when your anger frightens someone away from a dangerous situation so quickly that an accident is averted. (Yelling at a child might prevent its being run over.) The second is when you feel so furious about something that you fight to protect your very life, as in the case when you fight off hoodlums who are trying to rob you. Who cares whether or not your behaviour is called neurotic if your strategies have saved either someone else's life or your own?

Let us calmly react to irritating behaviour in a mature way, denying that (*a*) we have to have what we want, (*b*) those people who frustrate us are evil, and (*c*) that evil people are cured if you throw them into dungeons, beat them mercilessly, call them ugly names, and convince them that they are the scum of the earth. What kind of reaction would you expect from someone who is treated violently? Fear, for one. But hatred for another.

Fear

Under the heading of fear I include such emotions as worry, anxiety, nervousness, and panic. They are all forms of fear and vary in degree from the least intense — which is worry, to the most intense — which is panic. Fear and worry are created by two irrational ideas: (a) it is terrible and awful if things are not the way one would like them to be, and (b) if something is dangerous or fearsome, one should think about it, dwell upon it, and focus upon it endlessly in the belief that things will necessarily get worse.

You who are fearful persons see danger and threat in every situation, even in those that are clearly devoid of any danger. You convert a molehill into a Mt Everest. You get rejected, and you think it is the end of the world. If you don't get a promotion, you think it is a horrible experience. Someone steals your parking place, and you think it is a catastrophe.

When you describe events in such extreme terms: horrible awful, end of the world, unbearable, tragic, and catastrophic, you are setting yourself up for a nervous reaction. How else could you feel? Are you supposed to feel calm and serene when you describe what you are facing in such alarming terms?

Examine issues very carefully to see if the one you are facing is really as bad as you say it is. In the vast majority of cases you will find that you are exaggerating, that you are blowing things way out of proportion. This is an extremely common human tendency and is the cornerstone of all emotional disturbances.

What I am about to claim may sound like fantasy but consider it very seriously nevertheless. Would you like to know how never to get upset again for the rest of your life? Then take this advice: never made a catastrophe out of anything again and you will never be psychologically upset again. I know this is hard to believe, but stop and think a bit about how absolutely sensible and accurate that statement is. For example, if you were to describe a rejection as a regrettable event rather than as a horrible one, wouldn't you feel differently? Or if you thought of a demotion as a sad event rather than as a tragic one, wouldn't that make a difference to you? In other words, if you define or describe what happens to you in less alarming terms such as: regrettable, unfortunate, disappointing, sad, annoying, or irritating, you would feel simply *normally* frustrated. But when you describe them in drastic ways, you are not only going to be frustrated, you are going to be frightened, scared, nervous, and worried out of your skin.

Try to imagine how difficult it is for you to be calm and resigned to unfortunate events in your life (Rule 2) if you think that every bad event that happens to you is the end of the world. How can you tolerate something without being mightily upset if everything you don't like is a calamity? There is no way you can keep your stability and maturity and continue to carry on a pleasant relationship with someone if you are going to allow yourself to be destroyed emotionally because your perception of the entire event is way out of proportion? That is why the control of your fear is among the most important psychological tasks you need to learn.

Excessive passivity is unfortunately one of the forms of fear that destroys a great deal of happiness in very gentle people. Those of you who hate to assert yourselves are among the unhappiest of all persons I encounter. Yet, it is a pity that there are not more beautiful and giving people such as you. You do need to learn, however, not to be a coward when the need arises to stand up for yourself. I find there are five reasons why we act as cowards. Two of them are environmental and three are psychological.

The first reason why people behave as cowards is: they are afraid of being hurt physically. This makes good sense when you are facing a gorilla. If you know you are going to be pounded into the ground, run for your life. Nobody in his right mind wants to take on a physically superior opponent if he or she knows there is no chance of winning.

The second reason why we behave as cowards is: we are afraid of financial loss. The boss is always right. He writes out the cheques, and it is his business. If you don't like what he is asking you to do, quit. If you value your job don't argue with him too strenuously or you will find yourself out on the street.

The third reason we are timid and back off from our own convictions is that sometimes we are not sure of ourselves. We think, 'Wouldn't it be awful if I made a mistake?' Suppose you wanted to buy a house but your mate argues strongly against it. Since you can't know with certainty who is right, and because you have a great fear of being wrong, you give in to your lover's decision. In the end you wind up very seldom getting things to go your way. What is so wrong about being wrong? If you make a decision and it turns out to be an unwise one, so be it. One of the best ways to learn how to make sound decisions is to make many decisions. The more experience you get the more you are going to learn what to consider in making smart decisions. If you don't take the opportunity to learn by your errors, your partner does.

The fourth reason for not standing up for yourself is a fear of injuring the other person's feelings. After all, not giving people what they want often leaves them angry, depressed, hurt, resentful, and tearful. What you need to understand, however, is that you have not hurt that person's feelings. You can only hurt people physically, not emotionally. If someone wants to get depressed, angry, or nervous over one of your acts, that's *their problem,* not yours. They take that frustration and insist upon *converting* it into an emotional disturbance. Then they have the gall to turn around and say to you 'Look how you are upsetting me.' Your response should be 'Oh, I'm sorry dear, but you are doing this to yourself. Why don't you read a book, or go and talk to a clinical psychologist about your disturbance? I certainly don't want to see you disturbed every time I make a suggestion that you don't like. I hope you get over your problem very soon.'

And the fifth general reason why people do not assert themselves is: they fear rejection. They think rejection is painful, that it *has* to hurt, and that not being loved or approved by others is among the most horrible experiences in the whole world. Certainly being rejected hurts, but no more than you allow it to. All of you have been upset by the rejection of people whom you eventually didn't really much care about. At first rejection hurt, then you didn't care at all. Why is that? Because you convinced yourself that you didn't need that person's love and approval. Suppose you could have told yourself that immediately upon the first rejection? Can't you see how you would have been spared a lot of unnecessary pain?

If for a period of time, with a particular person, you are not having the kind of loving relationship that you want, it is hardly a catastrophe. It is not tragic; it is just regrettable. Do what you can to improve the situation and if it doesn't work, don't worry. There are always other people that one can love. It is also equally important to make sure people don't hate you. Those who can stab you in the back and are much more a cause of concern than someone who doesn't love you. So if you want to be greatly concerned about anything, be concerned about being hated, not unloved.

I have reviewed only briefly the self-defeating emotions that make it very difficult to achieve toleration without resentment (Option 1). If you want to be a mature and loving person despite the negative behaviour of another, you cannot achieve this goal if you are highly disturbed. To return goodness for evil you are required to be in control of yourself.

The weakest link: rational self-debate

In order to change your attitudes it is necessary to give more than just lip service to the need for change. It is essential that you examine your belief system so thoroughly that you are totally convinced that what you have been taught all of your life is probably incorrect and that these new rational views are much more sane. To do that, however, it is critical in dealing with frustrations that you do a great deal of challenging, debating, and analysing of your self-talk. You can make the assumption that, if you are still upset, you have not talked yourself out of your irrational nonsense. The only way you will know whether your debating over irrational ideas is working a change is when you feel relieved of the painful emotions that came from the irrational beliefs.

The major shortcoming most people have in their effort to become healthy emotional human beings is that they don't argue with themselves enough. They keep reinforcing such neurotic beliefs as: they must be perfect, it is terrible if they are not loved, people who behave badly are themselves bad, it is easier to avoid difficult tasks than it is to face them, and so on. Unless you argue with yourself against this nonsense, you are not apt to change. Debate, debate, debate with yourself until you become thoroughly convinced that you do not have to be perfect in order to be acceptable; you do not have to be loved in order to be acceptable. People are allowed to make mistakes and still be acceptable because they are not the same as their behaviour, and facing difficult tasks is easier than not facing them.

Study carefully the list of irrational ideas. It is critical that you convince yourself that they are silly and dangerous. And once you have done that, you are on the road to greater emotional control than you ever believed possible. Then you will be able to practise Rule 2: If someone does something bad to you, do something nice in return, for a *reasonable* period of time.

Who responds to rule 2?

There is a beauty and a majesty to returning goodness for evil. It is a noble and religious principle, one that has been prominent in the major beliefs of a number of religions. We have been taught that anyone, shown enough love, and given enough patience, will eventually react to our love and change for the better. Love is thus defined as nothing short of an endlessly giving process. If a sinner has not been changed by whatever we have done so far, we are encouraged to be patient, to pray, to see him or her as a child of God, and to have faith that our good actions will eventually soften those unfeeling attitudes.

The teaching that we should forgive those who trespass against us is so strong that we seldom ask ourselves how much we are expected to bear before we cease being tolerant. Unfortunately, people feel that when they forgive someone for an unkind act they are also not supposed to penalize them for it either. The teaching that we should forgive those who trespass against us does not say anything about not penalizing those who have injured us. Is it not possible to be completely forgiving and to be loving of those who do us wrong at the same time *because* we want to continue to love them, and to correct them for their wrongdoing? Forgiveness does not require that misbehaviour be accepted, only that we not hate the person because of the unacceptable act. In short, I can forgive my child for wrecking the car;

and even while I take her licence away, I can still be very fond and loving to her. Because I make her pay the damages and I do not let her have access to the car until she proves to be more responsible does not indicate that I hate her. Rather I demonstrate forgiveness and love on the one hand, and at the same time firmness and willingness to correct her behaviour.

Who responds well to the practice of reacting to bad behaviour with loving acts up to a point (Rule 2)? The answer is fairly obvious. It is the mature, the grown-up, the stable, and the emotionally untroubled person who benefits by our forgiving and loving behaviour. Troubled and immature people do not benefit from the generosity shown in Rule 2.

A mature person, when it is pointed out to him or her that some behaviour was unfair, readily responds with an apology and an attempt to make good. You are wasting your time, however, if it becomes clear after a time that your efforts are not working. When returning good for evil gets you nowhere, and you begin to sense, after several or many more trials, that things are actually getting worse rather than better, the only sensible conclusion you can come to is that you are dealing with a highly troubled or very immature person.

You can tell that your kind behaviour is backfiring (a) when your partner or child is not changing after a few trials, (b) when those persons seem not even to care enough to try to change, or (c) when they tell you outright that they have no intention of changing. What more do you need to know? Is not the handwriting on the wall? If you need more proof that returning good for bad is not working, then you have more of a problem than the other person does. It is obvious to any intelligent and reasonable person that Rule 2 (return good behaviour for bad for a reasonable period of time) is not working if no change actually occurs after a reasonable period of time. It is at this point that you may need to move on to Rule 3.

5

The last resort

What are you supposed to do when things get so bad with your family, friends, or employers that you feel you can no longer tolerate their inconsiderate behaviour? Surely anyone would agree there comes a time when patience runs out and tolerance reaches an end. As wonderful as it would be if we could have infinite patience and continue to love those who trespass against us, that is for most of us more of an ideal than a practical way of life. Only saints and martyrs can put up endlessly with injustices and manipulations. The rest of us are normally self-interested and simply are not able to tolerate rude, inconsiderate, and unjust behaviour for more than a reasonable length of time. But what do we do then?

We do what we have always done since the beginning of time. We rebel and fight back. In short, we follow Rule 3: If someone does something bad to you, do something bad to him or her (but without anger, and at first, with equal intensity).

Justification for Rule 3

If you have been raised to be a peaceful and co-operative individual, you certainly will not take kindly to this last piece of advice. There is something unpleasant and demeaning about the suggestion that we should return bad behaviour with bad behaviour. I feel as you do that it somehow goes against our higher sensibilities and our wish to be mature. Yet, what are you to do when reason does not work, when you have been patient, have gone the extra mile, have turned the other cheek, and have tried to sit down and discuss your mutual difficulties rationally, but nothing works? You would truly be a fool to keep on pursuing a strategy which is blatantly inefficient. Your only recourse is to make your frustrator *uncomfortable* until the offending behaviour has ceased or is sufficiently altered.

Remember the four options for dealing with frustration? Option 2, Protest, states that if you find that you cannot tolerate a situation without resentment, you should make a protest, go on strike, or declare a cold war until you get the changes you want. And if that does not work, you can always go back to Option 1,

Toleration without resentment. If you can't live with that, you can always go on to Option 3, Separation or divorce. Rule 3, reward bad treatment with bad treatment, deals with the second and third options. It says that the time for being nice is over and the time for being tough is beginning. When people step on your toes and won't stop doing it, then it's time for you to step on their toes. This downward spiral can continue until so much pressure is built up that someone may give in to preserve the relationship.

I feel that the resistance people will have against employing Rule 3 could be so strong in some instances that unless a clear justification is given, it will be difficult for that person to adopt it. Interestingly enough, it is the only one of the three rules which requires justification. No one quarrels over the notion that if one is treated nicely, it is quite appropriate to respond in an equally nice way. And few people would quarrel with the idea that if one is treated badly that it is inappropriate to immediately slaughter the other person. However, seriously to offer the advice that getting nasty with people who are nasty with us is clearly a whole new approach.

Yet, is it? Although Rule 2 admonishes us to forgive those who annoy us, don't forget that there is a great deal of similarity between some behaviour of our great religious leaders and Rule 3. Strange as it may seem to those who do not know the New Testament story, Christ used Rule 3. When he disapproved of the mercenary use to which the temple was being put by money lenders and merchants, he drove them out. Remember also that the Maccabean leaders of the Jewish people were strong and unyielding. They did not turn the other cheek. When pushed to extremes they fought back, they resisted, they made opposing armies very uncomfortable.

Gandhi did not, in a great gesture of tolerance, allow the British to dominate his nation. He was anything but yielding. Although he was non-violent, he was nevertheless difficult to deal with, uncooperative, and resistive in all ways. He annoyed the British government with his lack of co-operation for so long and so hard that eventually India won its independence.

And what about the American Black leaders in the last twenty-five years? Martin Luther King used Gandhi's methods with great success in acquiring greater civil liberties for the black people of the United States. His method was nothing short of the use of Rule 3. When the blacks were asked to move to the back of the buses, he led them to boycott the buses. There it is. That is the behaviour I am advocating; all of us use it when reason does not seem to have any effect on our frustrators.

If I have not convinced you yet that there is a justification for returning bad behaviour and, if my reference to religious leaders or civil rights leaders does not move you, then let me take you into the psychological laboratory. Remember how behaviour is influenced? If an act is rewarded or reinforced in any way, it becomes stronger. The likelihood of a person, a family, a group, or a corporation behaving a certain way depends upon whether or not a prior behaviour is rewarded or penalized. When an act is not rewarded, it tends to be weakened. From learning theory we also have the concept of extinction, which describes how human behaviour can be diminished or stopped.

All of these insights lead us to one conclusion: when behaviour continues to exist, it exists because it is rewarded. If we want change, and none occurs, we must conclude that the behaviour is *still being rewarded*. It may be we, or others, who are doing the rewarding. It may sometimes be difficult to determine who is reinforcing the behaviour and how that it is being done. Nevertheless, behaviour which continues to exist, exists because it is being reinforced.

It is time we fully appreciated this fact. All the good or bad which comes from humans is *our* responsibility. We are not responsible for earthquakes, storms or droughts; and trees, rocks and clouds are not responsible for people's behaviour. People are responsible for people's performances.

In greater or lesser degree it is we — you and I — who are responsible for poverty, war, crime, child abuse, and thousands of deaths each year on our highways. Why you and me? Because trees, rocks, clouds and rabbits, etc. don't cause war or divorces. Human behaviour is controlled largely by humans.

Therefore, logic clearly tells us if we want a behaviour not to continue, we had better stop reinforcing it. The one who is doing the reinforcing must stop that practice. This further means that if we want behaviour to change in someone else, *we must change first*. Closer examination often shows us that *we* are the ones who are creating our own headaches. We are forty-nine per cent responsible for what people do that we disapprove of because we tolerate these irritations so easily. The other parties are fifty-one per cent responsible because, in the final analysis, it is they who are behaving unacceptably.

Rationalizations for being passive

When you have tried your best to be gentle and persuasive in showing others how they are being inconsiderate, and you find that this does not work, it is more difficult than most people realize to go on to step 3, using the option of protest and strike. No one relishes the prospect of unpleasant confrontations that often can be long and drawn out. Confrontation can start ugly scenes and perhaps even rip a relationship apart. So, rather than take these chances, people will avoid conflict and use a number of rationalizations to justify this avoidance.

The first and most common excuse used by those who will not stand up for themselves is the fear of the fighting and yelling that often ensues when we put pressure on others to change. Nobody likes to change and the longer people have had their way, the louder they are going to squawk when they are made uncomfortable. Even when men and women are not violent and are not expected to become so, the possibility of their yelling, and saying ugly and nasty things strike fear in the hearts of most people. It seems as though they are about to be attacked with daggers.

I agree that all hell can break loose when you stop being the patsy you once were and you begin making other people somewhat miserable. However, it is easier to face difficult problems than it is to avoid them.

I agree with you that some unpleasant consequences are quite possible. What you may not understand, however, is that if you do not stand up for your rights at this point, if you feel that you cannot tolerate the situation without resentment, you do not have any other choice. I recommend you return negative behaviour with negative behaviour and teach that other person not to treat you so shabbily. In most instances what results is only a lot of angry talk. In the final analysis this cannot hurt you. Words do not hurt, no matter how nasty they are. A word is a vibration which comes from the other person's throat, passes the lips, sets air waves in motion, goes across the room, and lands on your ear drum. You are bombarded with these kinds of vibrations at all times; and unless they are literally of the intensity of an explosion, they are harmless. It makes no difference whether a person says, 'Fool', 'I hate you', or 'Witch'. These words are all harmless sounds landing on your ear. If you don't agree with those sounds, ignore them. If they happen to be true, acknowledge them and tell your partner that he or she is right and that you will do whatever you can to change because you don't want to be that way. But in most cases, of course, you will not feel that you are guilty of all the things you are accused of. So why should you be afraid of some noise? At sporting events or in a movie house we hear sounds that are many times louder than those you hear in an argument in your own kitchen.

Now you may complain that it is not the sound of the voice that bothers you but the meaning behind it. You fear that you are going to be rejected, unloved, and deserted. But does that usually happen? How many arguments have you had and the marriage did not dissolve? You will have to agree that it is a rare marriage that falls apart at the end of a single violent argument. In most cases it takes numerous disputes to rip a relationship apart. Therefore, in order to stop these fights, stop tolerating them.

A second reason why people make excuses for not wanting to move to Rule 3 is that they are afraid when they decide to become uncooperative they will hurt other people's feelings.

In our discussion of turning the other cheek, however, we learn that *you* cannot upset other people emotionally. If they want to get upset over your asserting yourself that is *their* problem. They don't seem to mind doing things you don't like, so why should you mind doing things they dislike? Even if your partner becomes depressed, I still insist that this is not something you are doing to anyone. It is what they are doing to themselves. As a matter of fact, when you begin to become somewhat difficult, you can usually expect a series of strategies from the other person to make matters worse and worse. They are done for your benefit, to weaken you and to make you back down.

Do not become frightened. Be prepared for the worst. But believe in the experiences of hundreds of people who have been amazed at how quickly others give in when they realize that none of their threats are going to work.

As a matter of fact, if you launch some handy counterattacks against the first assaults against you, you will be showing your partner in no uncertain terms that you are a changed person and are through tolerating the relationship the way it was.

Obviously, none of this is possible if you are always *over concerned* about the other person's feelings. Once you get over the inaccurate notion that you can hurt someone emotionally, you are capable of decisive actions. But as long as you believe that you are responsible for another person's feelings, you will never take the necessary steps. If you do not act, however, I assure you there will be a cold day in hell before you get that person's co-operation, respect, and love!

Words vs. actions

When your feelings warn you that you are reaching the end of your patience in any relationship you may wonder why the efforts you have attempted thus far have not brought relief. One common explanation for this disappointing state is that you may have assumed that the many discussions, complaints, and loud arguments constituted reasonable efforts on your part. What you may not realize is that talking is a strategy of returning good for evil (Rule 2). It directs you to sit down and reason with your friend, employer, parent, child, or lover. You may think you are applying Rule 3 when you argue loudly, but it is still one of the strategies of the second rule, not the third. Words belong to Rule 2, actions belong to Rule 3. It is time that you stop saying what you will do, and instead do what you say you will. There is an enormous difference between a word and an action even though there may be a great deal more heat created with an argument than there is with frustrating counter-behaviour.

If words and reasoning have not worked, my advice to you is to shut your mouth and *do* something about the situation. I find that people listen much better with their *eyes* than they do with their *ears*. Time after time in my practice I have come across men and women who were shocked into realizing how quickly their relationships were changed by a single, dramatic act by one party that instantly made an enormous impression on the other.

When people are sick and tired of complaining there are four actions they tend to take which bring their message home in unmistakable terms. The first is to see a lawyer. The second is to seek out a marriage counsellor. The third is to leave home. The fourth is to have an affair. These powerful actions require no further words to make an issue abundantly clear.

Acting instead of talking seems to be a difficult concept for people to grasp. Even when they finally do act, they think it is necessary to go back to the verbal level again and to explain why they have done what it is they have decided to do. They feel they must *explain* or *apologize* or *warn* over and over again. This is not so; an act is worth a thousand words. It says all that it is necessary to say: change, or the actions will become even more frustrating.

Do not back down once you have launched yourself on the road of protest. You are on strike. You have declared a cold war. The moment things get hot is the time when you will know that you are finally getting through to your frustrator. And you will not let up on this programme until you get the results you want.

The only thing you are interested in is that *behaviour must change*. How the excuse-makers will solve their problems is up to them. The woman with sex problems had better make a strong effort to overcome them or to get professional help. The man who has a drinking problem had better control it through sheer willpower or get the necessary help and learn to control it. We are not greatly interested in how they do it, *only that they do it*.

Other-pity is the great obstacle to the firmness it takes not to back down once you have embarked on a course of action. The moment you begin to feel sorry for the other person is the moment you weaken. Other-pity is the weak link in an otherwise strong chain which makes parents let a child watch television before he has finished his homework. Tears, arguments, and getting depressed are all common reactions the other person uses to play upon your sympathies. Remind yourself that the problem belongs to the other person and that he or she will only get worse if you don't take a hard-nosed attitude and stop making exceptions. To say, 'O.K. John, I'll let it go this time, but the next time you had better come in on time or I'll have to penalize you', is a meaningless threat unless you are really prepared to levy penalties. Actions convince people of what you mean, not words.

At times people's attempts to protest with *actions* rather than *words* wind up being very inefficient because the actions are more self-damaging than they are damaging to the other party. If you pressure others you certainly don't want to frustrate yourself too! Deciding to act instead of talk is going to cost you aggravation enough, I can assure you; making things additionally difficult for yourself is simply unwise.

Lowering ourselves to get even

If you have the same sensibilities that I, and I believe most people have, you will no doubt find carrying out Rule 3 rather distasteful. Not only are you required to go against your tender nature and no longer care excessively how others feel, but to make this programme work most effectively you will have to lower yourself to the level of your opponent. This is not easy for mature people. However, we are dealing with immature and troubled people. We have already learned that our treating them at a higher level only makes them worse. Unfortunately, when we approach them at a more civilized level we are not making ourselves understood. We conclude, therefore, that we must talk their language, and doing things to them similar to what they are doing to us, *is* talking their language.

The people around you may be shocked at the change in your behaviour, and they may well give in to you more quickly because they may conclude there is no way of changing your craziness. You will have to develop a thick hide to accomplish this because it is so out of character for you. This can be accomplished by not catastrophizing, not pitying yourself, and not pitying the other person.

Accepting Rule 3 does not mean that you will become insulting or angry, and thereby show yourself to be thoroughly immature also. You will only be acting in an uncooperative fashion because you are forced to for your sake and for the sake of the other person. I specifically want to emphasize this point: asserting yourself *never* has to be done with hatred or anger. In fact, assertiveness usually will not work if you allow yourself to become highly emotional and physically aggressive. It simply means that you will be difficult to get along with while at the same time you will be smiling and friendly. You will be detached and not over concerned over whether you are being loved in the process.

A good example of lowering yourself to the strategies of those who frustrate you would be to refuse to be sexually co-operative. Simply insist there will be no sex until things change to a reasonable degree.

All of us are assertive people, and the only difference between us is *when* we will decide to employ that assertiveness. I believe that we all can become intolerant of aggression if the cause is great enough.

If you think assertive behaviour is selfish, let me illustrate the meaning of two terms for you. (a) *Selfishness* is evident when a person wants something but does not feel obligated to repay the other party for making a sacrifice. Such people believe it is perfectly fine to receive benefits but not to give them. (b) *Self-interest* is evident when people are concerned about their own welfare but don't expect to be treated nicely without having to pay for it. Self-interested people reciprocate and expect a fair exchange of services. They receive but they are perfectly willing to give.

A woman who worked eight hours a day asked her husband to help with the dishes. He protested that this was woman's work and refused outright to co-operate. She asked me whether she was being selfish and I insisted she was being very self-interested instead. I suggested that she tell him that if he did not want to clean the dishes she would not cook. As a result they ate out numerous times, and she often purchased the more expensive items on the menu. After several lobster dinners he began to feel a pinch on his wallet, and he agreed to help her out after supper. This made her much easier to get along with and eventually they were all more happy than they would have been if she had allowed his uncooperativeness to continue.

There is no reason, however, for you to become any nastier than the situation warrants or more difficult than you need to be in order to get the results you want. Start off easily, and mildly. If this does not work, increase your resistance until you do get results.

How successful can such tactics be? I have already admitted that they certainly do not always work, but I must add that it surprised me and my clients how frequently they do. If you have a reasonable cause for complaint and you assert yourself without bitterness — just firmness, and if you stick with your cold war long enough, you may very well be surprised at how nicely things will change. People are really quite loath to break up a marriage. It generally takes an enormous dissatisfaction over a long period of time to bring a marriage relationship to the point of total non-co-operation. Before such a state is reached most people will give in.

Those of you who have certain religious prohibitions against separation and divorce will obviously have to tolerate more frustrations than those who don't have those prohibitions. You will have to learn to be less resentful, but more resigned, and hope that your good actions will eventually win over your partner by making him or her feel sorry for the bad treatment you are receiving.

The moral issue

I fully understand your reluctance to return harsh behaviour for harsh behaviour. As sensitive and caring people, we generally feel that it is ethically wrong to return one wrong for another. The old proverb that two wrongs don't make a right has a very convincing ring to it; and when I recommend that you kick others if they kick you, it would certainly seem as though I am urging you to commit a wrong as bad as the wrong that was done to you.

Such is not the case. When you do things to make others uncomfortable because you want to change their behaviour for the better, you have to realize that they are the ones who have indirectly urged you to use the harsher method. I hope that all along you were more than willing to use more gentle methods and that you are now only resorting to more extreme methods because the gentler approach did not work. You have reasoned, showed patience, turned the other cheek, and tried to be a very decent person about the whole matter, but this didn't work. Should you continue on that passive and tolerant course indefinitely? To do so would only encourage more misbehaviour.

Is it moral to fight evil, even if you have to use pain to do it? We assume that you are interested in changing someone else's unacceptable behaviour. To do so you must extinguish that behaviour by not rewarding it. That is the critical principle on which this whole argument rests. If you are eternally nice to someone who is mistreating you, then you are rewarding that person for being unkind. The only people who respond positively to your kind treatment are the unusually mature and stable ones; they can be shown with some patience that they are being unreasonable. The rest of humankind simply becomes programmed to become meaner and meaner.

To extinguish unacceptable behaviour, however, it is up to you to do something; you have to penalize it. You will want to make the offending person so increasingly uncomfortable by your actions that he or she stops. That is the fair thing to do. This is the opposite of rewarding your partner for being selfish. It is punishing him or her for being rude. It is therefore perfectly true to state that you are being tough with others to help them even though they can't appreciate what you are doing. They may feel that you are being very unfair, inconsiderate, and quite mean. But if your resistance is meant to get the person to give up a bad habit, then ultimately you may be helping that individual.

If you refuse to pick up the family's dirty clothing because they won't put it in a basket, and they thereby learn to be co-operative and put the dirty wash where it belongs, have you hurt them or helped them? If you leave your girlfriend at a party because she did not accept your warnings that you did not want her to flirt and drink too much, have you helped her? In my mind tough action with an offensive person is no different from taking a boy for a polio jab. Though the child may scream loud enough to be heard for miles, he still gets the jab because his mother or father knows very well what a very loving act it is to protect the boy against polio. We sometimes help those we love break bad habits that might eventually destroy our relationships with them and if this causes them some temporary discomfort, then that's still the way it has to be. We are interested in the *long*-range effects our negative behaviour may have. It becomes apparent then that it is well worthwhile to teach the family to be more responsible at home, teach the girl friend to conduct herself more properly if she wants your company, and teach the boy that a lifetime free from the threat of polio is worth a moment of pain. All are efforts to teach loving acts.

If you look at the issue in this manner, then I think you cannot fail to agree that being lenient and passive with people who are already behaving badly is an *immoral* act because it fosters more immoral behaviour. I further contend that you are not immoral even though you behave as your opponent does, because his or her act was prompted either by ignorance or disturbance, while yours is prompted by a desire to teach that person not to be either. The act may very well be the same but your *intention* is on a much higher plane.

It is high time that people begin to feel comfortable with their assertiveness. And if assertiveness does not work, then it is high time they became comfortable with their aggressiveness. The difference between those two approaches is that assertiveness is trying to get your way without force or violence; aggression is getting your way with force and violence.

You may protest that surely there must be a better way to deal with the human condition than to resort to increasingly negative behaviour until even violence is considered a moral position. I am afraid there is not. This reminds me of the protests that my couples in marriage counselling present to me when they too say that they wished they could do something other than what I am suggesting to them. Let me go over for you once more the choices we all have in facing unacceptable behaviour. And let me show you the dilemmas caused by all of these choices.

I first pointed out that one can usually tolerate a bad situation with grace. If you can't do anything about a bad situation, learn to resign yourself to it. My clients often say they have reached a point where they cannot tolerate someone anymore. So I offer them the next option: protest. They insist that this is something which bothers them too much and they do not want to sink to the other person's level. I suggest that they therefore leave the situation by a divorce or separation. 'Oh, but that's too upsetting, and besides, my religion doesn't allow it.' I then offer the fourth option which is to tolerate the situation with resentment, but to expect the usual emotional problems that follow. They naturally have no taste for this so I then say very seriously, 'Well, then why don't you tolerate it without resentment?' Then they point out that that is unacceptable, and around and around we go until they realize that all four choices are rather distasteful *and there are no other available*. A distasteful choice has to be made. Usually, the one they have the most hope for is trying to change the other person's behaviour, Option 2: protest. This is also one of the stormiest. But, if successful, it creates a condition that the person might actually live with. We sometimes learn the best when we are hurt the most.

Moral retardation

Consider this passage from The Bible. It comes from the Apostle Paul's *First Epistle to the Corinthians*, Chapter 13, verses 4–7, 'Love is patient and kind; it is not jealous or conceited or proud; love is not ill-mannered or selfish or irritable; love does not keep a record of wrongs; love is not happy with evil; but is happy with the truth. Love never gives up; and its faith, hope, and patience never fail.'

Were more elegant words ever written? Can you imagine what this world would be like if people lived up to its teachings? It has beauty, majesty, and hope; and we would like it to apply to all situations. Reasonable people, stable persons, and those who are not terribly troubled can accept this statement of love as a way of life. Those who are seriously troubled, or seriously immature, however, do not always respond to Paul's ideals. This way of love also does not seem to work with another class of persons whom I call: moral retardates.

Moral retardates are those who simply have a level of moral understanding that is far below what we would expect them to have in view of their ages and experiences. Just as one can give a score to people's intellectual performances, one can also approximate people's moral performance. Some individuals such as philanthropists might get a high score in moral behaviour. Petty individuals, torturers, hateful and nasty people, or those who mean well but who create needless pain for others would get low moral scores.

A moral retardate is somebody who is not necessarily disturbed or intellectually retarded. He or she is someone who is often quite intelligent, educated, and otherwise under at least average emotional control. Yet his or her moral development would be so deficient that it ranks at the retarded level when compared to the moral development of wise and compassionate people. It is this group that cannot be dealt with by Rule 2. They require the painful consequences of Rule 3 to make them change.

There are numerous examples of moral retardation that can be used to illustrate my point, but the most powerful I can think of is the prejudice that historically has been shown to blacks and to women. Blacks and females have both been treated unjustly by perfectly decent people in a white, male dominated society. Those who approved slavery and perpetuated discrimination, and the many males in our society who still think women should not have equal opportunities— these persons are normal, stable, and in many ways healthy moral people. Yet, they have committed injustices against millions. They are committing social injustices by violating the civil rights of half the population. But if they are so healthy and moral, why are they doing these things? Because in this area they are simply moral retardates. They do not see the immorality of their behaviour. They have not been trained to put themselves into another's place and to identify with their suffering lives.

Women have been abused, subjugated, and forced into second-class citizenship for thousands of years. And those who perpetrated these injustices were also respected, intelligent, sophisticated, and came from some of the highest and most respected institutions in the land. And they were moral retardates too, and that is why reasoning, patience, and turning the other cheek simply does not work with them. It is written that 'one should not suffer fools gladly'. I would like to amend that a bit and suggest we should not suffer mental retardates gladly either.

Fortunately we can alter this sad human condition and teach

people to be morally superior rather than retarded. And one of the ways to do it is to *return annoying behaviour for annoying behaviour*. This behaviour has actually been going on for centuries, and millions of people already practise it. But they do not understand that it has a very powerful moral base.

Consider the case of a woman who was abused by her alcoholic father for years to the point where she simply lost all feeling for him. She has forgiven him for his mistreatment but now wants nothing to do with him. Is she morally correct in her rejection? I believe she is. He earned her rejection. She does not have to be angry with him, nor hate him. He is not an unworthy person. He is simply a human being who had problems which no one was able to stop at the time. If she finds no pleasure in his company, it is his fault. Just because she does not hate the man does not mean she has to enjoy him or be of service to him.

Compare the above example of self-respect with the situation of a woman who told me that her husband treated her badly, emotionally and physically. She refused to punish him with even the slightest penalty for his abuse because 'He can't help it; he was an abused child.' As noble as she may at first appear to be, she is actually fostering more abusive behaviour by refusing to stop it. She is behaving neurotically. Long suffering individuals who tolerate from their mates all manner of behaviour including drunkenness, beatings, infidelities, and nagging, are usually not displaying profound acts of forgiveness. All too often they are simply self-loathing people who do not believe they deserve better treatment and, therefore, tolerate the most incredible unfairness from those closest to them.

A man once told me that his father forbade him ever to defend himself against children who might pick on him at school. He was a husky fellow and could easily have protected himself at any time, but he obeyed his father faithfully. The elderly gentleman went on the assumption that, (*a*) punitive behaviour was wrong no matter what the provocation and, (*b*) that eventually people would change. As a result, my subject was picked on and teased, shoved and hit by his schoolmates from the first grade to the twelfth. One day, in his senior year, he was thoroughly fed up with this injustice. He proceeded to beat up one of the worst offenders and shoved him into a hall locker. Was he right to do this? He should have been given a medal. How many more years did his father think he had to wait before he saw moral behaviour develop in the other children? President Theodore Roosevelt was certainly not far from the mark when he expressed Rule 3 in his own words 'Speak softly but carry a big stick.'

Obstacles to using Rule 3

Some people have such dissatisfying arrangements at work or in their marriages that separation of some kind is about the only sensible solution they can find. Yet, people who are in the most ridiculous kinds of marriages will also tell themselves that 'they don't believe in divorce'.

I once knew a man who was insanely jealous of his wife and made her live according to his rules and expectations to such a degree that she was an extremely unhappy woman. He successfully convinced her that divorce was immoral and totally unacceptable, and she was browbeaten enough to accept his arguments. She therefore made it possible for him to do whatever he wanted in his marriage. He could be impossible and inconsiderate and know that he would never lose his wife because a separation was unthinkable. How is anything to change if she doesn't have the ultimate weapon? Why should he change? He had *carte blanche* to abuse and dominate his wife without being the slightest bit affected by any pressure she might be able to exert against him.

But some people will not use Rule 3 and put pressure on their partners because they are afraid a divorce will demonstrate they have failed. Even though they may have been married for thirty-five years, they still think that a broken marriage is a failure. You have never failed in marriage as long as you have tried. If you have made marriage work for one week or fifty years you can always say you made it succeed for that period of time. If you couldn't or didn't want to carry it any further than that, simply because you knew it wouldn't work, you'd be sensible to leave.

It is about time we were taught to think with our heads and not with our hearts. I am sure there are times when we do not want to be superrational; we want our feelings to dictate our actions. No sensible person would offer the argument that it is always better to think like a computer in every instance. Life simply wouldn't be much fun because it wouldn't have much colour or excitement.

Do you want to know where the seat of power is in any relationship? Isn't it with the one who cares the least? If a relationship is too important to you, you are likely to give in too much to preserve it and to buy it at too great a price. If you are not excessively attached to something, however, you can deal with losing it much more easily; and you can drive a harder bargain. In a marriage this means that the one who cares for it the least, is going to get his or her way more often. The less caring person can always say 'If you don't like it, you can leave.' That's the way you would talk if your job were not terribly important to you. But if your very life depended on your job and the family were going to be put out on the street if you didn't have it, then they probably wouldn't rock the boat at any time for fear of the boss's disapproval. I find this highly unfair, but life is like that.

For years now I have been aware of the tendency to interpret most difficulties between parties as a result of poor communication. I have never agreed with that theory. In many cases a man and a woman will tell each other exactly how they feel and describe their problems at great length. Each knows the other person's reasons for his or her behaviour in all the detail that is necessary. Still they did not agree. Is it because they do not understand each other? Of course not. They understood each other completely but simply do not accept the other person's reasoning. This happens all the time between people and governments. What we have to understand is that sometimes we must *agree to disagree*. The belief that if we explain ourselves fifteen more times our listener will then understand us and agree with us is naïve.

George had spent his adult life being a decent human being. He worked at it consciously because he believed that sainthood was possible to achieve with great effort and resolute design. And he valued saintliness above all. To no one's surprise he became a minister, and in this profession he could pursue his ideals steadfastly. His charm, intelligence, and basic decency gained him respect and love from a wide circle, both inside or outside the congregation. His church was full, his popularity at its peak, and his good works unquestioned. So why did he need to see me?

Because he was falling out of love. The loss of feeling for his wife was growing, and he had not been able to reverse it. At times thoughts of divorce were so strong they shocked him. It troubled him deeply to realize that at times he could very easily turn his back on June, his wife of about fifteen years. Guilt over these reflections came naturally to his finely tuned sense of morality. He had promised to love her 'until death do us part'. But for two years he had struggled to push back the nagging truth that he wanted out.

He was fully aware of the impact this would have on his career. If it would not harm him greatly, it certainly would not help. His four children were at ages when divorce would be especially troubling to them. Above and beyond these problems was his belief that to move towards divorce would simply be in bad taste and poor form; and it was ethically unacceptable.

George wanted to change his wife, or himself, or both. It wasn't that he hadn't tried, that's not why he felt so exasperated. It was his lack of success. June's annoying habits surfaced slowly over the years. At first, shortly after George was ordained, she was still the light-hearted and fun-loving girl he courted. With every move up to a bigger church and a more prestigious congregation, however, June lost more of the joy of living and became more and more rigid. To cover her life-long insecurities she payed homage to the god of perfection. Anything less than the best in her children, husband, self, or home was unacceptable and viewed as a threat to her self-esteem. The inevitable consequence was clearly that she would become difficult to love and live with.

In our first session, George reviewed how he had coped with this problem.

'I tried to ignore her demands at first. Sometimes that worked rather nicely. Just as often, however, I'd find myself so annoyed at June's fussiness that I just couldn't hold back. Then we'd quarrel. I'd lose my cool and say things to hurt her. Then I'd feel guilty all day. I don't like being that way. It goes against everything I stand for.'

He went on to point out that he and the children 'have been walking on egg shells' to avoid her getting critical. Most of the time this maintained the peace. Every so often there would be minor explosions against her 'tyranny', but in a day or two tempers always cooled and the family would be stepping to her tune once more.

As nearly as I could determine, George resorted to verbal protests in reasoning with June. If he made himself clear once he made himself clear a thousand times. June knew precisely what he thought about kids coming home late, or getting average marks at school. He communicated his views on how it was perfectly fine to joke with her parishioners and their wives. She disagreed. To her, he lost their respect when he allowed them to treat him as an equal and to let everyone address him by his first name. This was a family that communicated quite well. That was seldom the problem. It was the lack of agreement which caused so much tension.

It seemed abundantly clear to me that he had relied too long on the gentle and persuasive methods of Rule 2 to change his wife. He repeated himself endlessly, trying to get his wife to understand an issue from his viewpoint as though she did not comprehend him.

Therapist: Why can't you see that she simply disagrees? Surely you can't think another year or two of giving her your reasons why you want her to change is going to succeed, do you?

Client: I'm almost sure you're right. God knows I've made my views known from every conceivable point. I just don't know how to convince her.

T: Why don't you stop being such a nice guy and give up your logical arguments for a few powerful acts?

C: Like what? You're not suggesting I get physical are you?

T: Certainly not, at least in the way you're thinking. But it is time for you to *do* something instead of *say* something.

C: Do what?

T: Any number of things. I'm not familiar enough with you or your wife to know what levers you can push.

C: Levers I can lower on her? I don't want to lower the boom on my wife. I want her to relax, stop being so blasted self-conscious and fussy with all of us and just enjoy life more.

T: I can't disagree with you. What you say makes a lost of sense. However, after years of trying to talk her into behaving as you prefer, what results have you got?

C: Not much.

T: Then isn't it about time you changed your strategy and stopped reinforcing her behaviour? Perhaps if you would stop being . . .

C: Excuse me for interrupting doctor, but what do you mean stop reinforcing her behaviour? Who's reinforcing her behaviour? I've fought it for years until I'm blue in the face.

T: You're rewarding her and thus reinforcing her ways. Why do you think she still acts this way after years of scolding her?

C: It certainly isn't because I condone it. You admit I've been giving her a bad time scolding her. So how can you think she's being encouraged?

T: If the behaviour exists, George, it exists because it's being rewarded. Behaviour which is not rewarded or reinforced is eventually extinguished.

C: But how can that be? I've never praised her for being constantly moody. I've never kissed her for yelling at the kids. And I've never hugged her for criticizing me for being friendly with members of my congregation.

T: I don't doubt that. Still, I insist, if people are behaving in a particular way towards you it's because you allow them to do so. If you didn't tolerate her annoying ways, she would either change, or you would resign yourself to them without resentment, or you would separate or divorce. Since she's doing the same annoying things to the family, I must conclude she's getting strokes from you for being annoying.

C: How? How can I possibly be giving her rewards while I'm doing nothing but protesting? I don't understand.

T: I think you just gave the answer. You were doing nothing but talk. Talk is cheap. Most people can let talk go in one ear and out the other. I suggest June was probably uncomfortable during those times *but*, not uncomfortable enough to change.

C: Even when I stormed out of the house at times, or when she left the room in tears?

T: Answer the question yourself.

C: Why do you ask me to do that?

T: Because the answer is obvious.

C: You mean, I suppose, that if nothing happened when I left, or when she cried, then she was still getting more pleasure somehow than the pain I gave her.

T: Precisely.

C: But where and how was the pleasure coming from?

T: Probably from her getting her way again. I suspect you yelled a lot but ended up giving in to her practically all the time.

C: But I had to. If I gave her too much opposition she'd reject me for days on end. There wouldn't be any affection and her anger at me would overflow on to the kids.

T: I'm sure that isn't pleasant, and I can understand why you'd want to avoid frustrating her.

C: You can say that again.

T: However, my point still stands. Whenever you ignore unacceptable behaviour, for whatever reason, it's likely to remain unchanged or get worse.

C: I've got to think this through. I know what you say makes sense, but it's hard to swallow.

I was attempting in this session and in subsequent visits to motivate him to give up being verbal and tolerant. Already he was a perfect example of dozens of people whom I have counselled who were no longer *just reasonably content*.

T: George, I don't want you to avoid doing something about June, because if you let her have her way at the cost of making yourself less than reasonably content you will actually be hurting yourself and the kids, as well as your wife.

C: I don't get it. How in heaven's name am I going to harm the whole family by giving June her way?

T: By bringing yourself below your JRC. That's the point where you're just reasonably content. Fall below that point and everyone is in trouble.

C: You mean that? If I'm badly frustrated, the whole family's in trouble?

T: I'm not talking about normal frustrations. I'm talking about chronic frustrations, the ones that go on for months and years. When you feel you're not even barely satisfied in a relationship, any kind of relationship, three bad things happen, George.

C: What are they?

T: First, you become upset, troubled, depressed, you bite your nails, or have nightmares, or drink, or have thoughts of infidelity.

C: I haven't had thoughts of cheating, thank God, but some of those other symptoms are definitely there. What are the other two points.

T: The second consequence of being chronically frustrated with a loved one is that you gradually but surely fall out of love. The third consequence is that you lose interest in the marriage itself.

C: I see. It seems that I've felt all three, wouldn't you?

T: That's the way I see it, yes. To prevent things from getting worse, you had better do something about reversing these results.

C: I see, or else you think I'll lose more feeling for June and eventually the marriage might end.

T: Right, if you ignore your own deepest desires and needs, June will feel great at first, but you'll get more miserable. Then she'll suffer too. I suggest you make her less content and make yourself more content.

C: What if she protests?

T: What if she does? In fact you can depend on her doing just that. However, your question is irrelevant. It makes no difference whether she's unhappy or not. The only thing I want you to focus on for the present is whether or not you're at the JRC.

C: Isn't it possible that I'll send June into a condition of low contentment if I pressure her to please me more?

T: Certainly.

C: Then what?

T: Then both of you can try using Option 1 and tolerate the frustrations without resentment. For example, you could talk yourself into not minding her nagging. Or she could do the same about your complaints.

C: I'm not sure we aren't past that point.

T: I suspect you are. So, as I see it, you're best off if you go on strike or declare a cold war until you get the kind of behaviour from June that will make you love her again.

He was beginning to see the strategy. In principle it met with his approval. In practice it bothered him considerably. Getting nasty with his wife went against his gentle nature.

C: I can't tell you how offensive I find your suggestion that I give June a bad time. The very thought of lowering myself to her immaturities bothers me. Her demands are bad enough without my acting just like her.

T: I sympathize with you completely. Look at it this way. If giving her a taste of her own medicine and making her uncomfortable when she becomes very unpleasant stops that behaviour, then what have you lost but a little pride? Remember, you tried for years talking to her with logic, reason, and patience and the result of trying to reach her on your higher level is that she's worse than ever while you're more unhappy than ever.

C: Yes, that's right. You said it.

T: So what do you have to lose if you communicate at her level? Speak her language and you may just get through for the first time.

C: I seriously doubt that this is going to work.

T: Why do you say that?

C: Because these tactics are going to raise such a stink that we're going to get into worse fights. The only thing that has helped this marriage is my backing down when she became demanding and loud. If I had not given in she would have become furious and I would have become so angry I'd say lots of things I didn't mean.

T: Oh, I see why you're hesitating. You're thinking your getting angry over her anger is like throwing petrol on her fire.

C: It certainly is.

T: But I wouldn't for one moment want you to be angry while you're trying to make her uncomfortable.

We then went into the psychology of anger in great detail. I pointed out to him that (1) only he makes himself angry, (2) he does it by thinking he has to have his way, (3) he thinks that people who frustrate him are bad, and (4) he wrongly believes that to change a bad person into a good person we have to be very punishing and hateful.

Between us we decided that ignoring her outbursts was the first step. We decided she'd get more upset for a time and put the marriage under it's greatest strain ever. However, I reasoned that if he held out and politely stayed out of her way and did his thing despite her protests, she'd see he was serious.

In the following weeks I coached him on how to frustrate her in hopes of breaking her bad habits and on how to do this calmly. For example, if she criticized him at a social function, he was to take her home there and then, after politely bidding the host and hostess goodnight.

If she made any purchase that cost more than the price to which they had agreed, he was to call up the store and have the item returned. If a cheque was already written for the item, he was to notify the bank immediately and stop payment. If she refused to spend a fair number of weekends and holidays with his parents, he was to refuse to visit hers.

She had a habit of keeping him waiting. When he felt the time of delay had reached the point of thoughtlessness, he was to tell her nicely he was going and that she could use her car to get herself to their appointment. He was not to argue with her, just give her a peck on the cheek, give her a smile, and say 'See you there soon, honey.' And then he was to leave without her.

C: That was one of the hardest things to do that you can imagine, I hated being so petty. Me, a minister, acting like a spoiled brat. Yet, since I'm paying her back in kind I want you to know things are definitely changing. I sense it every week. You told me she had no respect for me. Well, I'm slowly getting it now, and I'm very pleased. If I had known this years ago I'd never have let things go on so long.
T: Do you understand why you were so passive?
C: I've thought about that Dr Hauck and I think there are really two reasons. The first is that I didn't want to rock the boat and have my marriage in trouble. After all, I am a minister and I'm in

the business of counselling people. Well, you can imagine how it would look if I had a bad marriage or, worse yet, if I got a divorce.

T: What was your second reason?

C: The second is more a matter of principle. I have always been taught that love can conquer all. If people are not happy with each other we are supposed to love them, and accept them until they become more loving.

From what I've learned in therapy I can now see that love without demands can lead to emotional crippling, while being firm with our loved ones can be a very strong expression of love. We do that with our children, why shouldn't it work on an adult to adult level?

T: I couldn't have said that any better.

June eventually felt bothered enough that she wanted some control over all the 'crazy' things that were coming out of therapy. So she called to see me. I gave her about six sessions alone, and then we had a few more with George.

The results were most gratifying. George became less tolerant of June's unacceptable behaviour because he wasn't so worried about her leaving. This gave June a better feeling about him since she liked his strong hand. Incidentally, both seemed slightly surprised by this discovery. The relationship improved steadily. In fact, some of the lessons George learned in relating to June were later used in dealing with his children and even his church staff.

The most satisfying evidence of his change appeared in a couple of sermons incorporating his new views on co-operation respect, and love.

C: It wasn't easy to advise my people to show love through firmness because I knew they would regard that as revenge and reject it.

T: I can understand that easily though. It takes a lot of rethinking of old ideas to realize that giving people all they want can cause them not to respect or love us.

C: And that not being nice to a fault is the better way to love and be loved. However, I am still reluctant to act that way. Will I ever change?

T: It may get easier, but I think most people of good will are always going to feel reluctant when they are pushed to get tough. And I'm glad that's so. When we enjoy getting mean, we're in trouble.

C: Amen.

A realistic point of view

Much to my sorrow I have come to the conclusion that because of the nature of humankind, serious conflicts among us are inevitable. Violence and murder — even war — are inevitable. It appears that the only way these drastic outcomes can be avoided is if Rule 1 and 2 always work. That seems to me to be a far-fetched hope. It is highly unlikely that people and nations will always be so gracious as to reciprocate good deeds or to be patient and understanding when complaint is made against them. It is far more likely that in any dispute we will often not be able to see the correctness of the other person's position and will defend our viewpoint to the death.

It is ironic that a method which has such therapeutic value should also have such fatal consequences if overused. As I have tried to demonstrate, it is perfectly correct and scientifically sound to use penalties and punishments in order to rid people of objectionable behaviours. There is a delicate balance, however, between making people uncomfortable enough to cause them to change, and making them so uncomfortable they want to kill. No doubt the terrorists of the world would all claim that they have been pushed to the wall by a society that was deaf to their pleas. They would undoubtedly insist that their extreme tactics were necessary since all other methods failed. And believing that milder methods will be totally ineffective, they have felt pushed to use inhuman ones.

Is violence ever justified? Can violent acts be moral? Only if we could prove that violent measures are the only ones that work against an evil could we argue that evil means bring good ends. Our only hope for a sane world is that those who are in power have some sense of morality. If the good guys prevail, then Rule 3 will be used sparingly and cautiously. If the bad guys are in power we will have terror, war, and hell. Rule 3 is not a fault; the way it is used could be tragic. That is why I advocate the application of Rule 3 only as a last resort. It can contribute to loving relationships when employed lovingly.

Conclusion

I wrote this book because I felt compelled to do so. I have been dealing with people who have struggled with intimate relationships and were extremely unhappy over them. Some of the greatest suffering I have encountered on a daily basis has been with those who have not been happy at work, with families, or in their marriages. I have tried to understand the causes of this discontent and have come to formulate my reciprocity theory of love and my business theory of marriage; and I have formulated the three rules for achieving co-operation, respect, and love.

I have seen the lives of individuals change when they have looked reality squarely in the face and have followed these three steps whenever necessary and as far as necessary. I know that you too can face frustrations, change the behaviour of others, and bring a reasonable amount of happiness back into your life.

Try always to remember that too much other-pity can hurt those you love. Take the attitude, 'I love you enough to want to stop you from becoming the sort of person I can't tolerate.'

Remember that healthy love requires that you give to another all he or she *needs*, not all he or she wants. What we *need* is physical satisfaction and a roof over our heads. But there also are other kinds of needs — the need to be firm with others, the need to face challenges, the need to be tested by adversity, the need to take risks, and the need to face life with our own resources. Giving is unquestionably a loving act. Not giving, with the absence of a vengeful heart, can be the great love act of all.

Throughout life you can find how to love and be loved.

Index